OUTER SPACE

TAKE A FASCINATING JOURNEY THROUGH THE UNIVERSE

PaRragon

Bath·New York·Cologne·Melbourne·Delhi
Hong Kong·Shenzhen·Singapore·Amsterdam

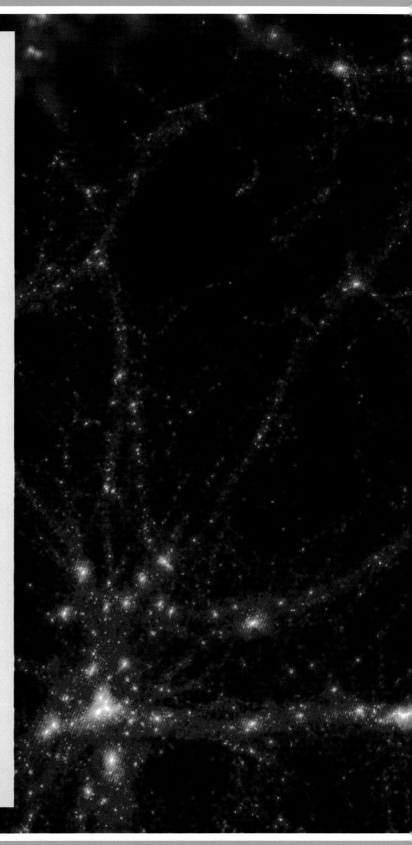

This edition published by Parragon Books Ltd
in 2015

Parragon Books Ltd
Chartist House
15–17 Trim Street
Bath BA1 1HA, UK
www.parragon.com

This edition © Parragon Books Ltd 2014–2015
© Original edition by Editorial SOL 90 S.L.

This edition produced by Jollands Editions
Cover design by JC Lanaway

ISBN 978-1-4723-7673-2

Printed in China

Based on an idea by Editorial SOL 90

Cover images courtesy of istock

Photography Corbis, ESA, Getty Images, AGE Fotostock,
Graphic News, NASA, National Geographic,
Science Photo Library.

CONTENTS

EAGLE NEBULA
This nebula, located 7,000 light-years from Earth, got its name from its shape, resembling an eagle with outstretched wings.

Introduction

Since the dawn of time, humans have been curious about what the heavens have to hide. It was this curiosity that led to the construction of telescopes and spacecraft, which have enabled distant objects – once blurry and vague – to be viewed with precision, and many astronomical phenomena to be seen for the first time. According to physics and mathematical calculations, the Milky Way contains up to four hundred billion stars. Our Sun is a resident of this galaxy, as is the Earth, which rotates around the Sun and is the only planet currently known to support life. Thanks to scientific and technological advances, human beings have been able to explore the far reaches of the Solar System and even beyond its boundaries. In doing so, some of the secrets of the Universe have been uncovered: its governing forces, its composition, its creation, the birth and death of stars, the features of black holes,

MAN ON THE MOON
An astronaut from the *Apollo 16* mission walks on the surface of the Moon, in a digitalized image made by Roger Ressmeyer from the original flight film.

the make-up of invisible dark matter that surrounds the galaxies and so much more. However, although space observation dates back to time immemorial, the history of space exploration is still very short. The first satellite was launched into space in 1957, and the space probe *Voyager 1* entered interstellar space in 2012, embarking on an unlimited journey through the Milky Way. In recent years, astronomers have started to observe other icy worlds, much smaller in size than planets, in a region known as the Kuiper Belt. Scientists affirm that the Kuiper Belt represents one of the most interesting moments in the exploration of the Solar System, given that a significant number of discoveries are now being made here. Orbiting spacecraft including *Mars Express* have confirmed the existence of ice deep inside the planet Mars. However, the search has only just begun; there is still a great deal to discover. For some time now, astronomers have been searching the Universe for other worlds similar to Earth, where life could be sustained. Perhaps one will be found farther away than we could imagine. Or perhaps, as some creative minds would like to think, the coming decades will see the project to colonize other planets come to fruition. For now, the best candidate is Mars. For the time being, however, this remains just a dream – like the one made reality on 21 July 1969, when man first set foot on the Moon.

The Moment of Creation

It is not known with any level of accuracy how, from nothing, the Universe was born. Initially, according to the Big Bang theory – the most commonly accepted theory among the scientific community – an infinitely small and dense hot ball appeared, which gave rise to space, matter and energy. This happened 13.7 billion years ago, although what generated it is unknown to this day.

AMAZING FACT

British astronomer Fred Hoyle (who disagreed with the theory) came up with the name 'Big Bang' when discussing it on a radio programme in 1949.

Energetic radiation

The hot ball that gave rise to the Universe was a permanent source of radiation. Subatomic particles and antiparticles annihilated one another; high density spontaneously created and destroyed matter. Had it remained in this state, the Universe would never have experienced the growth that, it is believed, occurred as a result of 'cosmic inflation'.

HOW IT GREW
The inflation caused each region of the young Universe to grow. The galactic neighbourhood appears uniform, with the same types of galaxy and the same background temperature.

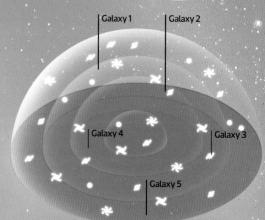

Galaxy 1
Galaxy 2
Galaxy 4
Galaxy 3
Galaxy 5

Time	0	10⁻⁴³ seconds	10⁻³⁸ seconds

Temperature	–	$10^{32}°$ C	$10^{29}°$ C

1 According to the theory, everything that currently exists was compressed into a space smaller than the nucleus of an atom.

2 At the moment closest to 'hour zero' that physics has been able to identify, the temperature is immensely high. A superforce governs the Universe.

3 The Universe is unstable and grows 100 trillion trillion trillion trillion trillion trillion times. Inflation starts and the forces separate.

ELEMENTARY PARTICLES
Initially, the Universe was a 'hotchpotch' of particles that interacted with others because of high levels of radiation. Later, once the Universe had inflated, quarks formed the nuclei of the elements, and with electrons, atoms were formed.

Photon
Light elementary particle with no mass.

Gluon
Responsible for interactions between quarks.

Electron
Negatively charged elementary particle.

Graviton
A particle believed to transfer gravity.

Quark
Light elementary particle.

The cosmic inflation theory

Big Bang theorists have been unable to understand with any level of certainty why the Universe has grown so quickly throughout its evolution. In 1979, physicist Alan Guth resolved this problem with his Inflation Theory. In an extremely short space of time (less than a thousandth of a second), the Universe grew 100 trillion trillion trillion trillion trillion times.

WILKINSON MICROWAVE ANISOTROPY PROBE

NASA's WMAP project mapped the Universe's background radiation, capturing the afterglow of the Big Bang 380,000 years after the event. The pattern of hotter (red–yellow) and cooler (green–blue) areas corresponds with the structure of galaxy clusters that would later evolve.

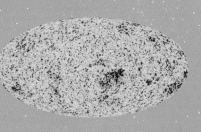

HOW IT DIDN'T GROW

If there had been no inflation, the Universe would have consisted of a series of clearly distinguishable regions. It would comprise 'remnants', each of which would contain certain types of galaxy.

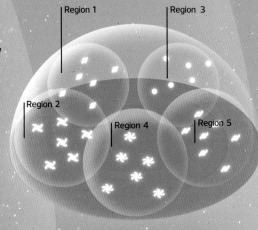

Region 1

Region 3

Region 2

Region 4

Region 5

SEPARATION OF FORCES

Before the inflation, there was just a single force that governed all interactions. The first to separate was gravity, then electromagnetic force and finally nuclear interaction. As the forces separated, matter was created.

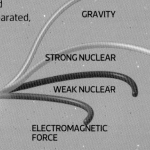

GRAVITY

STRONG NUCLEAR

WEAK NUCLEAR

ELECTROMAGNETIC FORCE

SUPERFORCE

INFLATION

10^{-12} seconds 10^{-4} seconds   5 seconds   3 minutes

$10^{15°}$ C

4 The Universe experiences an immense cooling process. Gravity becomes separated, electromagnetic force appears and nuclear interaction begins.

$10^{12°}$ C

5 Protons and neutrons are born, formed by three quarks each. The Universe is still dark: light is trapped in the mass of particles.

$5 \times 10^{9°}$ C

6 Electrons and positrons annihilate one another until the positrons disappear. The remaining electrons go on to form atoms.

$10^{9°}$ C

7 They create the nuclei of the lightest elements: helium and hydrogen. Each nucleus comprises protons and neutrons.

1 second Neutrinos decouple as a result of neutron disintegration. With a very small mass, neutrinos go on to form most of the Universe's dark matter.

FROM PARTICLE TO MATTER

Quarks interacted with others thanks to the force transferred by gluons. Later, along with neutrons, they formed nuclei.

Quark

Gluon

1 A gluon interacts with a quark.

2 Quarks join gluons to form protons and neutrons.

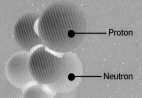

Proton

Neutron

3 Protons and neutrons join to form nuclei.

The transparent Universe

The creation of atoms and general cooling allowed the Universe, which was dense and opaque, to become transparent. Photons, light particles with no mass, were free to roam space; radiation lost its crown as governor of the Universe, and matter was able to carve out its own destiny under the forces of gravity. Gaseous accumulations grew, and over hundreds of millions of years formed protogalaxies; thanks to gravity, they became the first galaxies, and in denser regions, the first stars began to fuse hydrogen and release energy. The great, lingering mystery is why the galaxies took on their current shape. Dark matter – an intergalactic empty space – could hold the key; it was responsible for their expansion and can only be detected indirectly.

1 Gas cloud
The first gases and dust generated by the Big Bang formed a cloud.

2 First filaments
As a result of dark matter's gravity, gases joined together to form filaments.

DARK MATTER
Dark matter, invisible to the most powerful telescopes, makes up 23 per cent of the Universe, and a mysterious dark energy accounts for 73 per cent. Galaxies and stars move as a result of the gravitational effects of dark energy and matter.

EVOLUTION OF MATTER
The Big Bang initially produced a gas cloud that was uniformly dispersed. Three million years later, the gas started to organize itself into the shape of filaments. Today, the Universe can be seen as networks of galactic filaments with enormous spaces between them.

TIME	**380,000** years	**500 million**

TEMPERATURE	**2,700°C (4,892°F)**	**–243°C (–405°F)**

8 Atoms are born. Electrons orbit around the nuclei, attracted by protons. The Universe becomes transparent. Photons travel throughout space.

9 Galaxies acquire their definitive shape: 'islands' with billions of stars and masses of gas and dust. Stars explode as supernovas, and scatter heavier elements such as carbon.

FIRST ATOMS
Helium and hydrogen were the first elements to be joined at an atomic level. They are the main components of stars and planets, and the most common throughout the Universe.

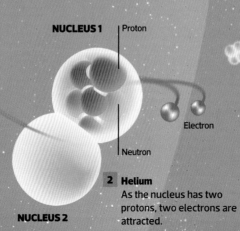

NUCLEUS 1 | Proton

Electron

Neutron

NUCLEUS 2

1 Hydrogen
An electron is attracted and orbits around a nucleus, which contains a proton.

2 Helium
As the nucleus has two protons, two electrons are attracted.

3 Carbon
Over time, more complex elements like carbon (six protons and six electrons) were formed.

3 Networks of filaments
The Universe can be seen as filaments with billions of galaxies.

The Universe today

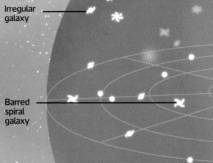

Nebula

Irregular galaxy

Star

Spiral galaxy

Quasar

Barred spiral galaxy

Elliptical galaxy

Galaxy cluster

9.1 billion

THE EARTH IS CREATED
Like all the other planets in our Solar System, the Earth was formed from material left over from the creation of the Sun.

9 billion

13.7 billion

–258°C (–432°F)

10 Nine billion years after the Big Bang, the Solar System is born. A mass of gas and dust collapses, giving rise to the creation of the Sun. Then, with the remaining material, a planetary system is brought together.

–270°C (–454°F)

11 Currently, the Universe continues to expand, with a vast number of galaxies separated by dark matter. The predominant energy is an unknown – dark energy, which acts as a kind of antigravity.

AMAZING FACT

Located in a 1.6-km (1-mile) deep former gold mine in South Dakota, the Large Underground Xenon (LUX) experiment is designed to detect dark matter.

COSMIC CALENDAR

In an attempt to make the magnitudes of time related to the Universe more tangible, US writer Carl Sagan introduced the concept of the 'Cosmic Calendar'. On 1 January of that imaginary year, at 12:00 am, the Big Bang occurred. *Homo sapiens* would appear at 11:56 pm on 31 December, with Columbus discovering America (in 1492) at 11:59 pm that same day. One second in the Cosmic Calendar is representative of 500 years.

Big Bang
Occurred on the first second of the first day of the year.
JANUARY

The Solar System
Created on 24 August in the Cosmic Calendar.

Columbus arrives in America
This would occur on the last second of 31 December.
DECEMBER

The Stars

For a long time, stars were a mystery to humankind. Today, it is known that they are enormous spheres of plasma, mostly hydrogen with a smaller amount of helium. Based on the light they emit, experts can ascertain their brightness, colour and temperature. Given their huge distance from Earth, they can only be seen as dots of light, even with the most powerful telescopes.

GLOBULAR CLUSTER
Around 10 million stars together form the largest cluster in the Milky Way: Omega Centauri.

OPEN CLUSTER
The Pleiades are a formation of around 1,000 stars that will scatter throughout space in the future.

Hertzsprung–Russell Diagram

The H–R diagram groups stars according to their visual brightness, the spectral type that corresponds to the wavelengths of light they emit, and their temperature. Stars in the Main Sequence with a greater mass tend to be brighter – they include blues, red giants and red supergiants. Stars live 90 per cent of their lives in the Main Sequence.

Light-years and parsecs

In order to measure the immense distance between stars, the terms light-year (ly) and parsec (pc) are used. A light-year is the distance light travels in one year: almost 9.5 trillion km (6 trillion miles). A pc is the distance between the Sun and a star if its parallax angle is one arc second. One pc equals 3.26 ly, or 31 trillion km (19.3 trillion miles).

AMAZING FACT

The hottest stars (O-, B- and A-spectral type) are blue-white in colour. The coldest (G-, K- and M-type) stars are yellow, orange and red.

O-TYPE
(40,000 to 29,000°C)

B-TYPE
(29,000 to 9,700°C)

A-TYPE
(9,700 to 7,200°C)

F-TYPE
(7,200 to 5,800°C)

G-TYPE
(5,800 to 4,700°C)

K-TYPE
(4,700 to 3,300°C)

M-TYPE
(3,300 to 2,100°C)

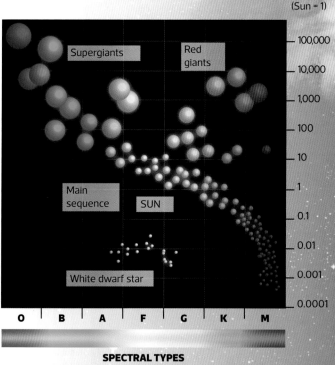

VISUAL BRIGHTNESS (Sun = 1)

Supergiants

Red giants

— 100,000

— 10,000

— 1,000

— 100

— 10

— 1

Main sequence

SUN

— 0.1

— 0.01

White dwarf star

— 0.001

— 0.0001

O B A F G K M

SPECTRAL TYPES

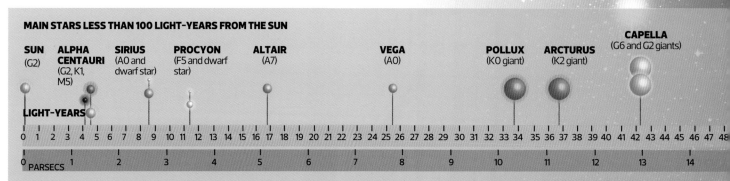

MAIN STARS LESS THAN 100 LIGHT-YEARS FROM THE SUN

SUN (G2)

ALPHA CENTAURI (G2, K1, M5)

SIRIUS (A0 and dwarf star)

PROCYON (F5 and dwarf star)

ALTAIR (A7)

VEGA (A0)

POLLUX (K0 giant)

ARCTURUS (K2 giant)

CAPELLA (G6 and G2 giants)

LIGHT-YEARS

0 1 2 3 4 5 6 7 8 9 10 11 12 13 14 15 16 17 18 19 20 21 22 23 24 25 26 27 28 29 30 31 32 33 34 35 36 37 38 39 40 41 42 43 44 45 46 47 48

0 PARSECS 1 2 3 4 5 6 7 8 9 10 11 12 13 14

Measuring distance

When the Earth orbits the Sun, the nearer stars appear to move over a background of more distant stars. The angle that results from the movement of a star within the Earth's six-month rotation period is known as the 'parallax angle'. The closer a star is to Earth, the larger the parallax.

The parallax angle of star A is smaller because it is a long way from Earth.

The parallax angle of star B is greater than that of A. B is therefore closer to Earth.

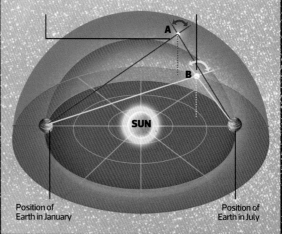

SUN

Position of
Earth in January

Position of
Earth in July

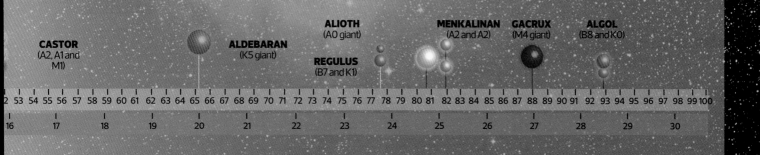

CASTOR
(A2, A1 and
M1)

ALDEBARAN
(K5 giant)

ALIOTH
(A0 giant)

REGULUS
(B7 and K1)

MENKALINAN
(A2 and A2)

GACRUX
(M4 giant)

ALGOL
(B8 and K0)

The Evolution of Stars

Stars are born in nebulae – enormous gas clouds, mainly consisting of hydrogen and dust, that float in space. They can live for millions, or even billions, of years. Often, their size can provide clues about their age: smaller stars tend to be younger, while larger stars are closer to perishing, soon to cool down or explode as supernovas.

Massive star

More than eight solar masses

1 **Protostar**
Comprising a dense, gaseous core surrounded by a dust cloud.

2 **Star**
The star is born. Hydrogen fuses to form helium during the main sequence.

Nebula

A cloud of gas and dust collapses because of the effects of gravity; it heats up and divides into smaller clouds that may form protostars.

Low-mass star

Fewer than eight solar masses

The life cycle of a star

The evolution of a star depends on its mass. Low-mass stars, like the Sun, have much longer, more modest lives. When they run out of hydrogen, they turn into red giants and, eventually, end their lives as white dwarves until they completely burn out. Stars with a greater mass eventually explode: all that is left of one is a superdense remnant – a neutron star. Significantly more massive stars eventually form black holes.

1 **Protostar**
Formed by the release of gas and dust. Its core rotates owing to the effects of gravity.

2 **Star**
It shines and slowly consumes its hydrogen reserves. It fuses helium while it grows in size.

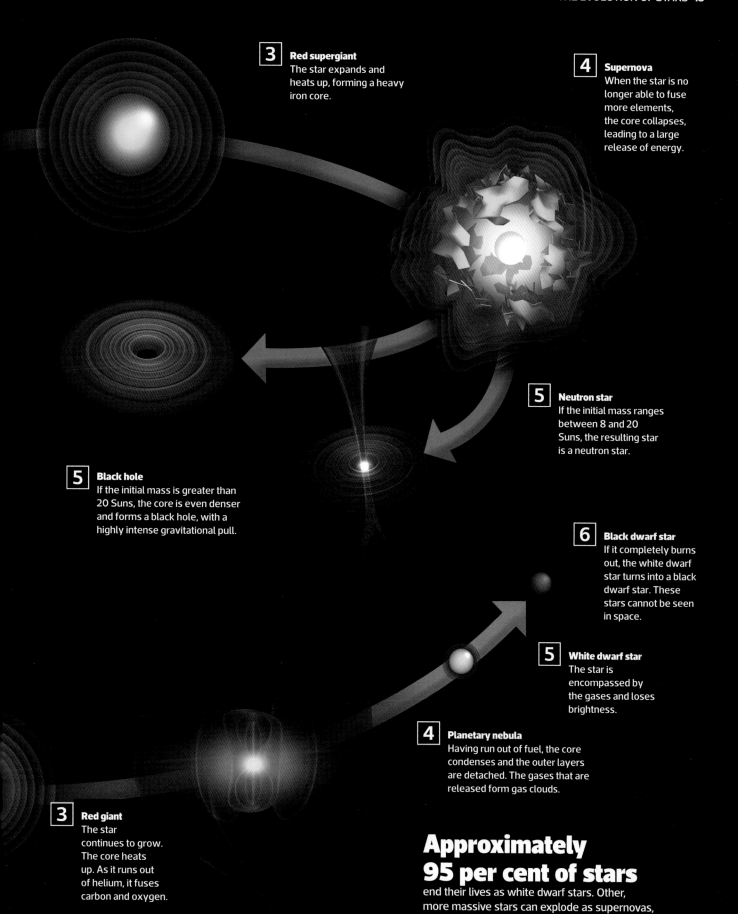

3 Red supergiant
The star expands and heats up, forming a heavy iron core.

4 Supernova
When the star is no longer able to fuse more elements, the core collapses, leading to a large release of energy.

5 Neutron star
If the initial mass ranges between 8 and 20 Suns, the resulting star is a neutron star.

5 Black hole
If the initial mass is greater than 20 Suns, the core is even denser and forms a black hole, with a highly intense gravitational pull.

6 Black dwarf star
If it completely burns out, the white dwarf star turns into a black dwarf star. These stars cannot be seen in space.

5 White dwarf star
The star is encompassed by the gases and loses brightness.

4 Planetary nebula
Having run out of fuel, the core condenses and the outer layers are detached. The gases that are released form gas clouds.

3 Red giant
The star continues to grow. The core heats up. As it runs out of helium, it fuses carbon and oxygen.

Approximately 95 per cent of stars
end their lives as white dwarf stars. Other, more massive stars can explode as supernovas, illuminating entire galaxies for weeks.

Planetary Nebulae

When low-mass stars die, they leave behind only enormous shells of expanding gas; these are known as 'planetary nebulae'. When early astronomers viewed them through telescopes they could see discs that looked like planets; the name has stuck ever since. In general, they are symmetrical and spherical objects. When viewed through a telescope, a white dwarf star – a remnant of the original star – can be seen at the centre of several nebulae.

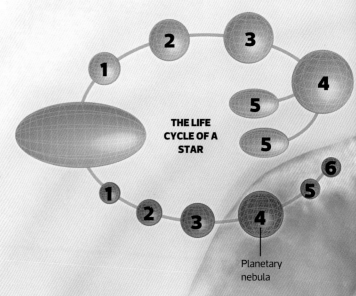

THE LIFE CYCLE OF A STAR

Planetary nebula

◀M2-9

Also known as Minkowski's Butterfly, this tiny planetary nebula contains two stars that orbit around one another within a disc of gas that measures ten times the size of the orbit of Pluto. It is 2,100 light-years from Earth.

CONCENTRIC CIRCLES

Spheres of gas form an onion-layer structure around the white dwarf. The mass of each white dwarf is greater than all the masses of the Solar System's planets combined.

AMAZING FACT

The surface temperature of a white dwarf star is twice that of the Sun. This is why it appears white, despite its brightness being a thousand times less.

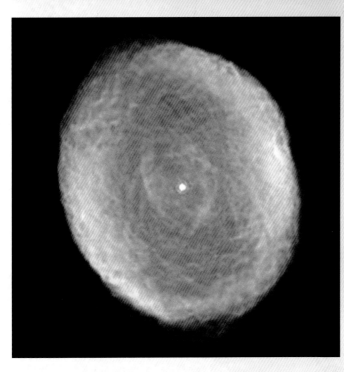

◀IC 418

The Spirograph Nebula has a hot, bright core that has stimulated neighbouring atoms, making them glow. Located 2,000 light-years from Earth, it measures 0.3 light-years in diameter.

HYDROGEN

Constantly expanding gaseous masses are mostly made up of hydrogen, in addition to helium and, to a lesser extent, oxygen, nitrogen and other elements.

3 tons

This is what one spoonful of a white dwarf star would weigh. In size it would look similar to a spoonful of ice cream, but its mass would be vastly different. The mass of a white dwarf star is immense, despite its diameter – about 15,000 km (9,300 miles) – being comparable to the diameter of the Earth.

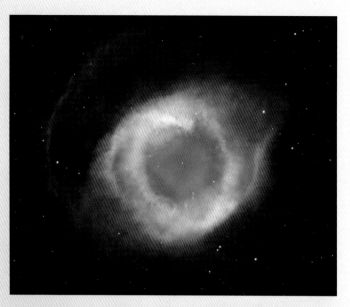

NGC 7293 ▶

The Helix is a planetary nebula created at the end of the life of a star similar to our Sun. It is 700 light-years from Earth.

MYCN 18 ▶

Two rings of gas form the silhouette of the Hourglass Nebula. The red colour corresponds to nitrogen, and the green colour to hydrogen. This nebula is 8,000 light-years from Earth.

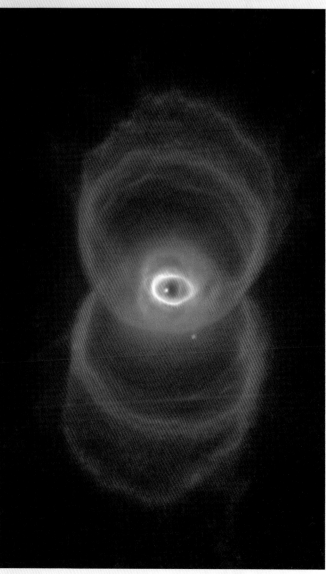

WHITE DWARF STAR
The remainder of the red giant can be found at the heart of the nebula. The star cools down and, at some stage, completely extinguishes; as a result, it becomes a black dwarf star and can no longer be seen.

GREATER DIAMETER
Less massive white dwarf

SMALLER DIAMETER
More massive white dwarf

Density of a white dwarf

The density of a white dwarf is one million times greater than the density of water. In other words, one cubic meter of a white dwarf star would weigh one million tonnes. The mass of a star varies, and is indirectly proportional to its diameter. A white dwarf star, with a diameter 100 times smaller than the diameter of the Sun, has a mass 70 times greater.

Supernova

The explosion of a massive star towards the end of its life is extraordinary. There is a sudden increase in its brightness and an enormous release of energy. This is a 'supernova', and it releases, in just ten seconds, ten times more power than the Sun will release in its entire life. After the star's detonation, a gaseous remnant remains, and this expands and shines throughout the galaxy for millions of years.

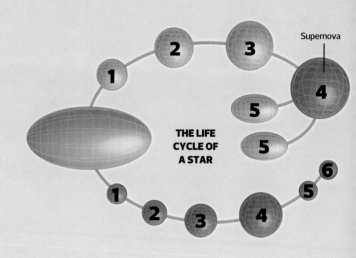

THE LIFE CYCLE OF A STAR

Supernova

A star's decline

The explosion that sees the end of a supergiant's life is attributable to its extremely heavy iron core no longer being able to support its own gravitational pull. As internal fusions are no longer possible, the star collapses in on itself, expelling the remaining gases outwards; these then expand and shine for millennia. The expelled elements provide the interstellar medium with new material, which is capable of giving rise to new generations of stars.

AMAZING FACT

It is estimated that two supernovas explode each century in the Milky Way, but the last one visible with the naked eye occurred in 1604.

CORE
Divided into different layers, each one corresponds to the different elements generated as a result of nuclear fusion. The final element created prior to the collapse is nuclear iron.

Fusion
The nuclear reactions happen more quickly than those of a red giant.

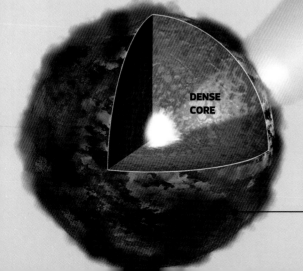

DENSE CORE

SUPERGIANT
Once the star swells, it is capable of measuring more than 1,000 times the diameter of the Sun. The star is capable of producing elements heavier than carbon and oxygen.

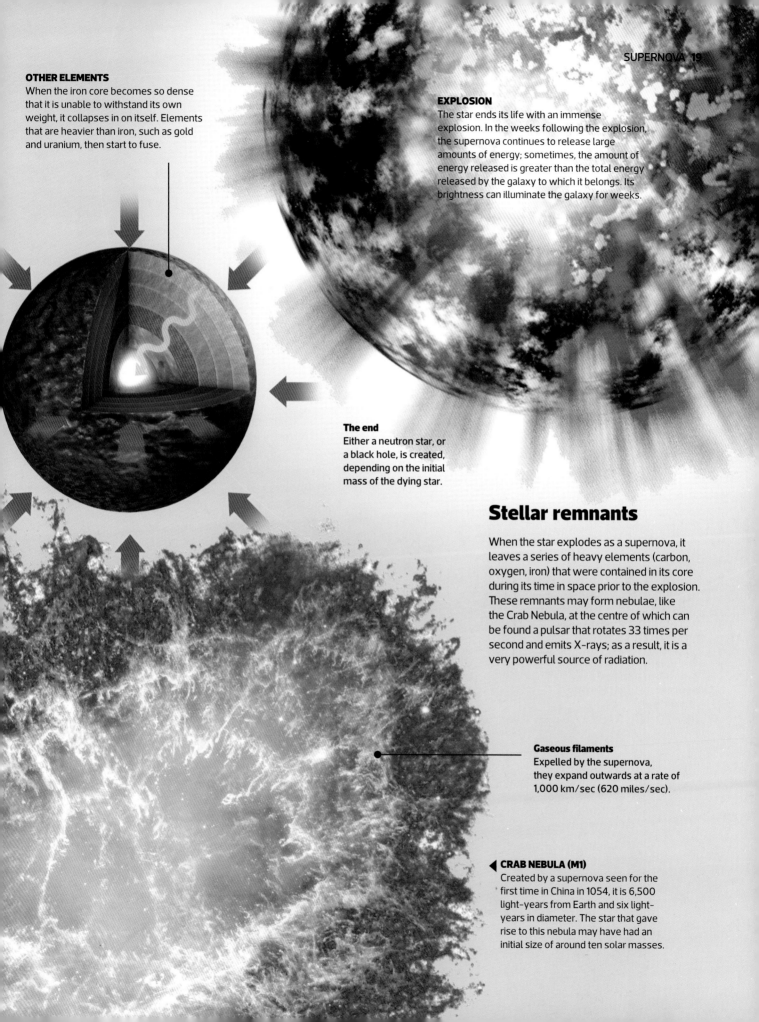

OTHER ELEMENTS
When the iron core becomes so dense that it is unable to withstand its own weight, it collapses in on itself. Elements that are heavier than iron, such as gold and uranium, then start to fuse.

EXPLOSION
The star ends its life with an immense explosion. In the weeks following the explosion, the supernova continues to release large amounts of energy; sometimes, the amount of energy released is greater than the total energy released by the galaxy to which it belongs. Its brightness can illuminate the galaxy for weeks.

The end
Either a neutron star, or a black hole, is created, depending on the initial mass of the dying star.

Stellar remnants

When the star explodes as a supernova, it leaves a series of heavy elements (carbon, oxygen, iron) that were contained in its core during its time in space prior to the explosion. These remnants may form nebulae, like the Crab Nebula, at the centre of which can be found a pulsar that rotates 33 times per second and emits X-rays; as a result, it is a very powerful source of radiation.

Gaseous filaments
Expelled by the supernova, they expand outwards at a rate of 1,000 km/sec (620 miles/sec).

◄ CRAB NEBULA (M1)
Created by a supernova seen for the first time in China in 1054, it is 6,500 light-years from Earth and six light-years in diameter. The star that gave rise to this nebula may have had an initial size of around ten solar masses.

The Death of a Star

The final stage in the evolution of a star's core is the formation of a very compact object, the nature of which depends on the mass that collapses. More massive stars end up as black holes; these strange objects have such intense gravity that not even light can escape.

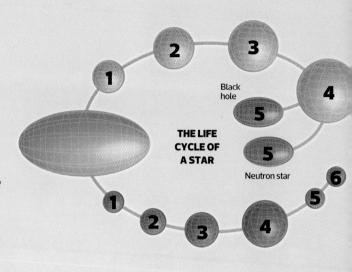

THE LIFE CYCLE OF A STAR

Black hole

Neutron star

Black holes

Black holes have intense gravity, and nothing that gets too close – not even light – can escape. This means they are very difficult to detect, although measuring unusual effects on nearby objects gives astronomers clues that a black hole may be present: 1) Objects orbiting or spiralling into a black hole provide mass estimates. 2) Intense gravity from a black hole can bend light, known as 'gravitational lensing'. 3) Material falling into a black hole heats up and forms an accretion disc, which glows so brightly that it can be detected from Earth.

X-rays
Gas enters the black hole and is heated up. This results in the emission of X-rays.

LIGHT RAYS

ACCRETION DISC
An accumulation of gases that a black hole absorbs from neighbouring stars. The gas spins at an extremely high speed and, in areas very close to the black hole, this results in the emission of X-rays.

Darkness
Like any other object, light is trapped if it passes very close to the core.

Neutron star

When the initial star has a mass of between 10 and 20 solar masses, its final mass will be greater than that of the Sun. Despite having lost significant amounts of matter during the nuclear reaction process, the star ends up with a very dense core, resulting in the creation of a 'neutron star'.

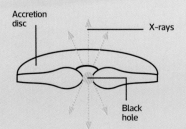

1 billion tons

is the weight of one spoonful of a neutron star. Although the size is similar to the spoonful of chocolate spread shown (left), its mass is vastly different. It has a compact and dense core, with an intense gravitational pull.

1 Red giant
Its diameter is 100 times greater than the diameter of the Sun.

2 Supergiant
It grows and quickly fuses elements. It produces carbon and oxygen until it finally forms iron.

4 Dense core
Its exact composition is unknown. It contains interacting particles, most of which are neutrons.

3 Explosion
The iron core collapses. Protons and electrons annihilate one another to form nuclear neutrons.

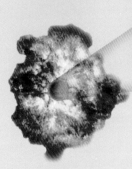

Full escape
When light passes very far from the centre, it follows its natural course.

Close to the limit
Light has still not crossed the event horizon, the limit between what is and what is not absorbed, and it maintains its brightness.

SHINING GASES
As the accretion disc feeds on the gases that spin at extremely high speeds, the part closest to the core shines intensely. Towards the edges, it has a colder and darker appearance.

CROSS SECTION

Accretion disc

X-rays

Black hole

Pulsars

The first pulsar to be discovered was found in 1967. Pulsars are neutron stars that emit radio waves; they rotate between 30–716 times per second and have a very intense magnetic field. A pulsar emits waves from both its poles as it spins. If it absorbs gas from a neighbouring star, it generates a heat spot on its surface that emits X-rays.

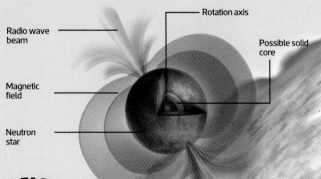

Rotation axis

Radio wave beam

Possible solid core

Magnetic field

Neutron star

AMAZING FACT

Scientists have shown that large galaxies have a black hole at their centre. These are 'supermassive' black holes, with masses greater than one million Suns.

DEVOURING THE GAS OF A SUPERGIANT
Located in a binary system, a pulsar is capable of following the same process as a black hole. Faced with a neighbouring star with a smaller mass, by means of its gravitational pull it absorbs the star's gas, heating its surface. Thus, the pulsar is capable of emitting X-rays.

The Milky Way

For many centuries our own galaxy, the Milky Way, so named because of its milky, band-like appearance in the night sky, was a true mystery. It was Galileo Galilei who, in 1610, directed his telescope onto it and saw that the dim cloudy-white band comprised thousands and thousands of stars, practically stuck to one another. Gradually, astronomers started to realize that all the stars, and our Sun, formed part of one large entity: a galaxy, our huge stellar home.

Structure of the galaxy

Our galaxy has two spiral arms that rotate around the core. It is on these arms that the youngest objects in the galaxy can be found, and where interstellar gas and dust are most abundant. On the Sagittarius Arm, one of the brightest stars in the Universe can be found – Eta Carinae. Our Solar System is located on the inner border of the Orion Arm, between the Sagittarius and Perseus Arms.

ROTATION
The speed at which the Milky Way rotates does not vary greatly depending on the distance from the core. One circuit of our Sun around the centre of the galaxy (a cosmic year) is estimated to take approximately 225–250 million years.

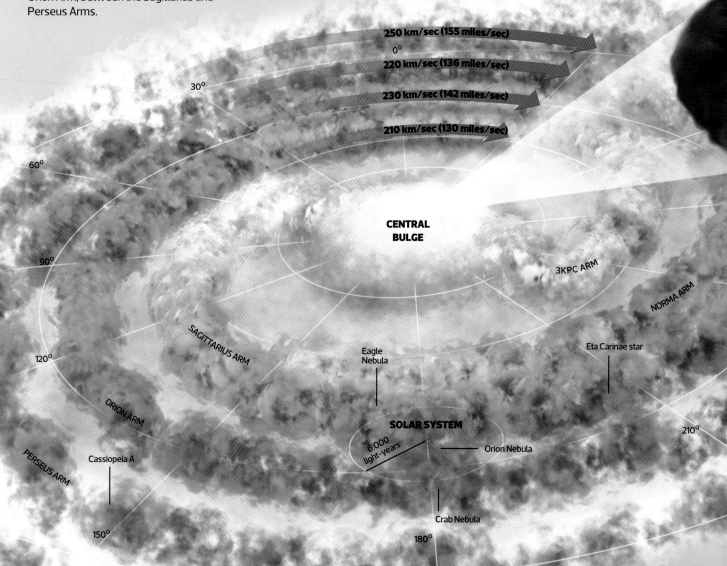

250 km/sec (155 miles/sec)
0°
220 km/sec (136 miles/sec)
30°
230 km/sec (142 miles/sec)
210 km/sec (130 miles/sec)

60°

90°

120°

150°

CENTRAL BULGE

3KPC ARM

NORMA ARM

SAGITTARIUS ARM

Eta Carinae star

Eagle Nebula

ORION ARM

210°

SOLAR SYSTEM

6,000 light-years

Orion Nebula

PERSEUS ARM

Cassiopeia A

Crab Nebula

180°

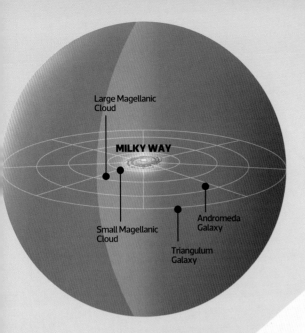

Large Magellanic Cloud

MILKY WAY

Small Magellanic Cloud

Andromeda Galaxy

Triangulum Galaxy

Hot gases
Emitted from the surface of the central part. They may be the result of violent explosions on the accretion disc.

Shining stars
They are created from gas that is not swallowed by the black hole. Most are young.

Gaseous vortexes
From the centre outwards, the gas is held and concentrated by a gravitational force that may be attributable to a black hole.

Black hole
One is believed to occupy the centre of the galaxy. It attracts gas through its gravitational pull and keeps it in orbit.

AMAZING FACT

Obscured by gas and dust clouds, the shape of the galaxy's centre was not clearly known until the 1990s, when it could be viewed using infrared radiation.

Magnetism
The heart of the galaxy is encompassed by a region with strong magnetic fields, perhaps resulting from a rotating black hole.

Sagittarius B2
The largest dark cloud in the central area.

Outer ring
A ring of smoke and dark dust molecule clouds expands as a result of a huge explosion. It is suspected that this was attributable to a small object towards the centre.

CARINA ARM

240°

OUTER ARM

Central region

The central axis of the galaxy contains old stars, dating back around 14 billion years, and exhibits an intense level of activity at its interior. Here, two hot gas clouds can be found: Sagittarius A and B. In the central region, although outside the core, a giant cloud contains 70 different types of molecule. These gas clouds are attributable to violent activity at the centre of the galaxy. The heart of the Milky Way can be found in the depths of Sagittarius A and B.

100–400 billion
stars inhabit the Milky Way. The number it contains is so high that they cannot be separated in this image.

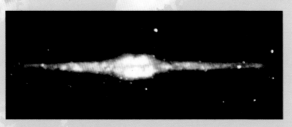

◀ The appearance of the Milky Way

If we could see it from the side, our galaxy would look like a flattened disc with a bulge towards the centre. Around the disc there is a spherical region, called the 'halo'; here, there are globular clusters of stars and dark matter.

The Solar System

The planets, satellites, asteroids, other rocky objects and the vast number of comets that circle the Sun comprise the Solar System; its diameter is often considered to be in the region of two light-years. The elliptical paths of the planets around the Sun are known as 'orbits'. Today, thanks to advances in astronomy, over 1,000 extrasolar planets have been confirmed, and there are doubtless many more waiting to be discovered.

Types of planet

Our Solar System is home to eight planets that orbit a single star: the Sun. Those closer to the Sun are rocky, smaller planets, whereas the more distant are gaseous, larger planets.

Outer planets

The outer planets are located outside the asteroid belt. They are huge balls of gas with small, solid cores. Their temperatures are extremely low, because of the huge distance that separates them from the Sun. The greatest in size is Jupiter, into which Earth would fit 1,300 times.

NEPTUNE   **URANUS**   **SATURN**

The creation of the planets

The first proposals suggested that the planets were gradually formed by hot dust particles that joined together. Today, scientists believe that they were generated by the collision and merger of two or more larger bodies, known as 'planetesimals'.

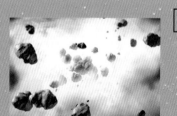

1 **Origins**
The remnants from when the Sun was created generate a disc of gas and dust, from which planetesimals form.

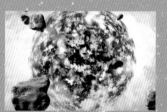

2 **Collision**
When they collide, the planetesimals of different sizes join together with other objects that have a greater mass.

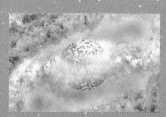

3 **Heat**
These collisions generate a significant amount of heat inside the planets, depending on their distance from the Sun.

AMAZING FACT

The word 'planet' comes from the Greek for 'wandering star', because ancient astronomers watched these bodies moving around in the night sky.

SOLAR GRAVITY
The Sun's gravitational pull on the planets does not just keep them within the confines of the Solar System, it also influences the speed at which they orbit. Those closer to the Sun orbit more quickly than those farther away.

Inner planets

They are solid bodies inside which occur geological phenomena, such as volcanism, that are capable of changing their surface. Almost all have a palpable atmosphere, although varying in thickness; this plays a key role in the surface temperature of each planet.

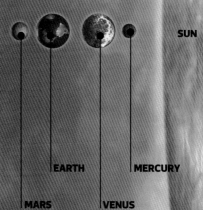

SUN

EARTH

MERCURY

MARS

VENUS

Asteroid belt

The boundary between the inner and outer planets is defined by an assembly of millions of rocky fragments of different sizes, which form a ring known as the 'asteroid belt'. Its movement is seen to be influenced by the gravitational pull exercised by Jupiter.

JUPITER

The Sun

The Sun is an enormous ball of plasma (superheated gas). It is mainly hydrogen (90 per cent) and helium (9 per cent), with traces of elements such as carbon, nitrogen and oxygen, among others. To humankind, it is a vital source of light and heat; this energy is produced by the fusion of hydrogen atomic nuclei.

CONVENTIAL PLANETARY SYMBOL FOR SUN ⊙

ESSENTIAL DATA

Average distance from Earth 150 million km (93 million miles)	
Diameter at the equator 1.4 million km (865,000 miles)	
Orbital speed 220 km/sec (135 miles/sec)	
Mass (Earth = 1) 332,900	
Gravity (Earth = 1) 28	
Density 0.255 g/cm³	
Average surface temperature 5,500°C (9,950°F)	
Atmosphere Dense	
Moons No	

NUCLEAR FUSION

1 Nuclear collision
Two hydrogen nuclei (protons) collide and fuse to create a nucleus of deuterium, releasing a neutrino, a positron and a significant amount of energy.

2 Photons
The deuterium formed collides and fuses with another proton, and a high-energy gamma-ray photon is released. It will take many thousands of years to reach the photosphere.

3 Helium nucleus
A group of two protons and a neutron collide with one another. A helium nucleus is formed, and a couple of high-energy protons are released.

CONNECTIVE ZONE
This extends from the base of the photosphere to a depth of around 15 per cent of the solar radius. Here, energy is transported outwards by (convective) currents of gas.

RADIATIVE ZONE
Particles from the core cross this zone. A proton could take up to a million years to cross it.

8,000,000°C (14,400,000°F)

15,000,000°C (27,000,000°F)

CORE
It occupies just 2 per cent of the Sun's total volume, but is responsible for around half of its total mass. Because of the intense pressures and temperature, thermonuclear fusions are generated here.

Positron

Proton

Neutron

Neutrino

Deuterium

Photon

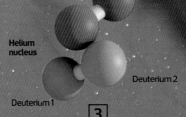

Helium nucleus

Deuterium 2

Deuterium 1

Proton 1

Proton 2

Surface and atmosphere

The visible portion of the Sun is a ball of light, comprising boiling gases that emanate from its core. The flares of gas form plasma that crosses this layer. It then penetrates a vast layer of gases called the 'solar atmosphere'; here, two strata, the chromosphere and the corona, overlap. The energy generated by the Sun's core moves through the surface of the photosphere and the atmosphere for thousands of years.

Sunspots
These are areas of gas that are cooler (4,000°C/7,000°F) than the photosphere (5,500°C/9,950°F); as a result, they are darker in appearance.

CHROMOSPHERE
Above the photosphere, and with a much lower density, this 5,000-km (3,000-mile) thick layer ranges in temperature from 4,500°C to 500,000°C (8,000–900,000°F), depending on the distance from the core.

500,000°C
(900,000°F)

Spicules
These rising vertical jets of gas are attributable to the chromosphere. They often reach 10,000 km (6,000 miles) in height.

Macrospicules
These types of vertical jet are similar to spicules, but they often reach a height of 40,000 km (25,000 miles).

CORONA
Located above the chromosphere. It extends millions of kilometres into space and reaches extremely high temperatures.

1,000,000°C
(1,800,000°F)

Solar prominences
Clouds and layers of gas from the chromosphere that reach the corona. As a result of the activity of the magnetic fields to which they are subjected, they take on the form of an arc or a wave.

5,500°C
(9,950°F)

PHOTOSPHERE
This is the visible surface of the Sun, a boiling, thick tide of gases in a state of plasma. Density decreases while transparency increases in its outermost stratum. Thus, solar radiation escapes into extrasolar space in the form of light.

Solar flares or protuberances
These jets are released from the solar atmosphere and are capable of interfering with radio communication on Earth.

AMAZING FACT

The Sun is an almost perfect sphere, and its mass makes up 99.86 per cent of the total mass of the Solar System.

Mercury

Mercury is the closest planet to the Sun, and as a result areas of the surface can reach a temperature of 425°C (800°F). It moves at a high speed, orbiting the Sun every 88 days. It has practically no atmosphere and its surface is dry and harsh, scarred by numerous faults and by craters caused by the impact of meteorites.

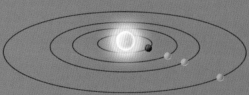

CORE
Dense, large and made of iron, its diameter is believed to measure between 3,600 and 3,800 km (2,200–2,400 miles).

A scar-covered surface

On Mercury's surface, it is possible to observe craters of different sizes, flatlands and hills. Recently, evidence of frozen water was found in the polar regions of Mercury. The polar ice may be located at the bottom of very deep craters, preventing the ice from interacting with sunlight.

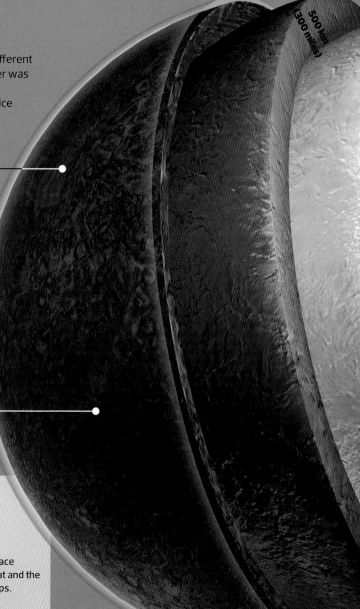

500 km
(300 miles)

3,600 km
(2,200 miles)

Caloris Basin
Measuring 1,550 km (960 miles) in diameter, it is one of the largest craters in the entire Solar System. (The largest is Utopia Planitia on Mars, with a diameter of 3,300 km/2050 miles.)

The crater was submerged in lava.

When the projectile that formed the crater made impact, Mercury was still being formed: the radiating waves created hills and mountains.

Rembrandt
The planet's second biggest crater is 715 km (445 miles) in diameter.

MEAGRE ATMOSPHERE
Mercury's atmosphere is almost nonexistent: it consists of a very fine layer that is unable to protect the planet from the Sun or meteorites. As a result, the surface temperature varies enormously between day and night.

During the day, the Sun directly heats the surface.

At night, the surface quickly loses heat and the temperature drops.

425°C
(800°F)

–173°C
(–279°F)

Composition and magnetic field

Like Earth, Mercury has a magnetic field, although it is much weaker (around 1 per cent of Earth's). The magnetism is attributable to its huge core, which is composed of solid iron. The mantle that encompasses the core is made from a fine layer of liquid iron and sulphur.

29 per cent sodium

22 per cent hydrogen

43 per cent others

6 per cent helium

CONVENTIONAL PLANETARY SYMBOL FOR MERCURY

ESSENTIAL DATA

Average distance from the Sun	57.9 million km (36 million miles)
Solar orbit (Mercurial year)	88 days
Diameter at the equator	4,880 km (3,032 miles)
Orbital speed	47.87 km/sec (29.75 miles/sec)
Mass (Earth = 1)	0.06
Gravity (Earth = 1)	0.38
Density	5.43 g/cm³
Average temperature	167°C (333°F)
Atmosphere	Almost nonexistent
Moons	None

AXIAL TILT

0.1° One rotation lasts 59 days.

MANTLE
This mantle mostly comprises silicate-based rocks.

CRUST
Made from silicate rocks and similar to Earth's crust and mantle. It ranges between 500 and 600 km (300–375 miles) thick.

Rotation and orbit

Mercury spins slowly on its axis and takes approximately 59 calendar days to complete a full turn, but needs just 88 to travel its orbit. To an observer on Mercury, the combination of these two movements would result in an interval of 176 days between two sunrises.

MERCURY'S ORBIT AROUND THE SUN

Each number corresponds to a position of the Sun in the sky, as seen from Mercury.

3 It reaches its zenith (midday) and stops.

4 It moves backwards slightly.

VIEW OF THE SUN FROM MERCURY

6 It resumes its path until it reaches the horizon.

5 It stops again.

2 It climbs and its size increases.

7 It falls towards the sunset.

1 The Sun rises.

HORIZON OF MERCURY

Venus

Venus is the second closest planet to the Sun. Similar in size to Earth, it has a volcanic surface and a hostile atmosphere, and is ruled by the effects of carbon dioxide. Four billion years ago, the atmospheres on Earth and Venus were similar; today, the air pressure on the surface of Venus is 92 times that of the Earth. Its sulphuric acid and dust clouds are so thick and dense that it would be impossible to see the stars from the planet's surface.

AMAZING FACT

Galileo's observations of the phases of Venus, which are only possible because it orbits the Sun, were among his proofs that the Earth is not the centre of the Universe.

The effects of its thick atmosphere

The predominant carbon dioxide content in Venus's atmosphere generates a greenhouse effect that elevates the planet's surface temperature to around 462°C (864°F). Consequently, Venus is hotter than Mercury, despite being farther from the Sun and the fact that only 20 per cent of sunlight reaches its surface (because of its dense atmosphere). Atmospheric pressure on Venus is 92 times greater than the pressure on Earth.

80 km (50 miles)

is the thickness of Venus's atmosphere.

MANTLE
Comprising molten rock, it is responsible for trapping solar radiation.

CORE
Believed to be similar to Earth's core, with metallic (iron and nickel) and silicate elements. It has no magnetic field, perhaps because of its slow rotation speed.

CONVENTIONAL PLANETARY SYMBOL FOR VENUS ♀

ESSENTIAL DATA

Average distance from the Sun 108 million km (67 million miles)	
Solar orbit (Venusian year) 224 days 17 hours	
Diameter at the equator 12,100 km (7,520 miles)	
Orbital speed 35.02 km/sec (21.76 miles/sec)	
Mass (Earth = 1) 0.8	
Gravity (Earth = 1) 0.9	
Density 5.25 g/cm3	
Average temperature 462°C (864°F)	
Atmosphere Very dense	
Moons No	

AXIAL TILT

177.3°
One rotation (retrograde) takes 243 days.

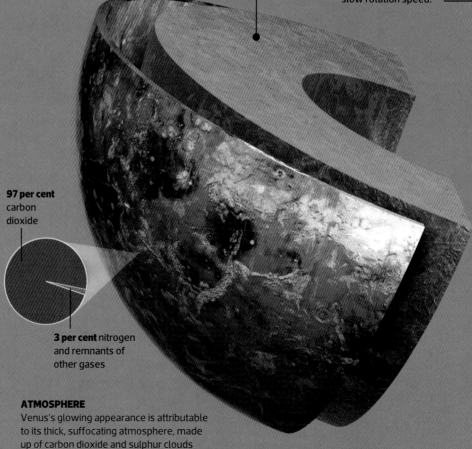

97 per cent carbon dioxide

3 per cent nitrogen and remnants of other gases

ATMOSPHERE
Venus's glowing appearance is attributable to its thick, suffocating atmosphere, made up of carbon dioxide and sulphur clouds that reflect the Sun's light.

Phases of Venus

While Venus orbits the Sun, its visibility from Earth is greater or less depending on its position compared with the Sun and our planet. That is to say, it has 'phases' like those of the Moon. It is brightest during elongations (the angle between the Sun and the planet, as viewed from Earth) when it is farthest from the Sun in the sky. At these times, it can be seen after the Sun sets or before it rises.

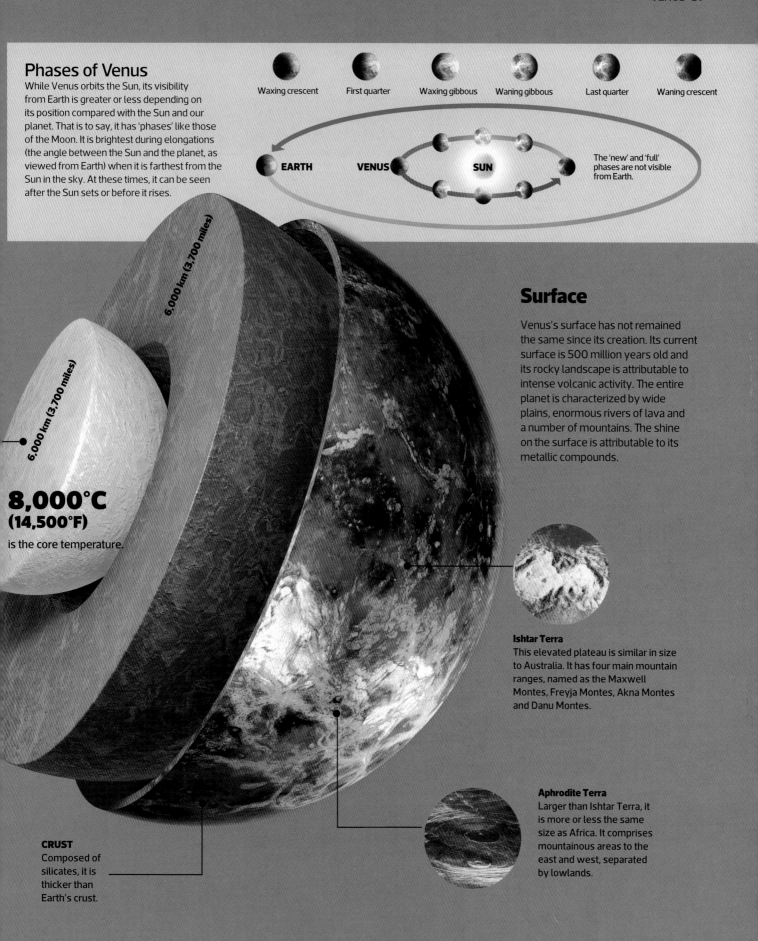

Waxing crescent   First quarter   Waxing gibbous   Waning gibbous   Last quarter   Waning crescent

EARTH   VENUS   SUN

The 'new' and 'full' phases are not visible from Earth.

6,000 km (3,700 miles)

6,000 km (3,700 miles)

8,000°C
(14,500°F)
is the core temperature.

Surface

Venus's surface has not remained the same since its creation. Its current surface is 500 million years old and its rocky landscape is attributable to intense volcanic activity. The entire planet is characterized by wide plains, enormous rivers of lava and a number of mountains. The shine on the surface is attributable to its metallic compounds.

Ishtar Terra
This elevated plateau is similar in size to Australia. It has four main mountain ranges, named as the Maxwell Montes, Freyja Montes, Akna Montes and Danu Montes.

Aphrodite Terra
Larger than Ishtar Terra, it is more or less the same size as Africa. It comprises mountainous areas to the east and west, separated by lowlands.

CRUST
Composed of silicates, it is thicker than Earth's crust.

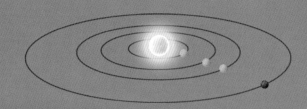

Mars

Known as the 'Red Planet', because its surface is covered in iron oxide, Mars's atmosphere is thin and not particularly dense; it is essentially composed of carbon dioxide. Its orbital period, tilt axis and internal structure are all similar to those of Earth. Its poles house ice pockets, and although no water can be seen on its surface, it is believed that the planet's water content was high in the past, and that there may be water in the sub-surface.

Martian orbit

Mars's orbit is more elliptical than Earth's; as a result, its distance from the Sun varies more. At its closest point, Mars receives 45 per cent more solar radiation than at its farthest point. Surface temperatures vary between -140°C and 17°C (-220°F and 63°F).

-140°C (-220°F)
in winter

17°C (63°F)
in summer

MANTLE
Molten rock, the density of which is greater than Earth's surface.

Moons

Mars has two moons, Phobos and Deimos, both of which are more dense than Mars and pockmarked with craters. They consist of carbon-rich rock. Deimos orbits Mars in 30.3 hours, whereas Phobos, which is closer to the red planet, does so in just 7.66 hours. Astronomers believe that the moons were asteroids attracted by Mars's gravity.

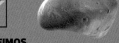

DEIMOS
Diameter 15 km (9.3 miles)
Distance from Mars 23,458 km (14,576 miles)

PHOBOS
Diameter
27 km (16.8 miles)
Distance
from Mars
9,376 km (5,826 miles)

AMAZING FACT

The diameter of Mars is 6,794 km (4,222 miles), making it almost half the size of Earth and the second smallest planet in the Solar System.

ATMOSPHERE
Its thin atmosphere consists of carbon dioxide and features clouds, weather systems and prevailing winds.

95.3 per cent
carbon dioxide

2.1 per cent
oxygen, carbon monoxide, water vapour and other gases

2.6 per cent
nitrogen

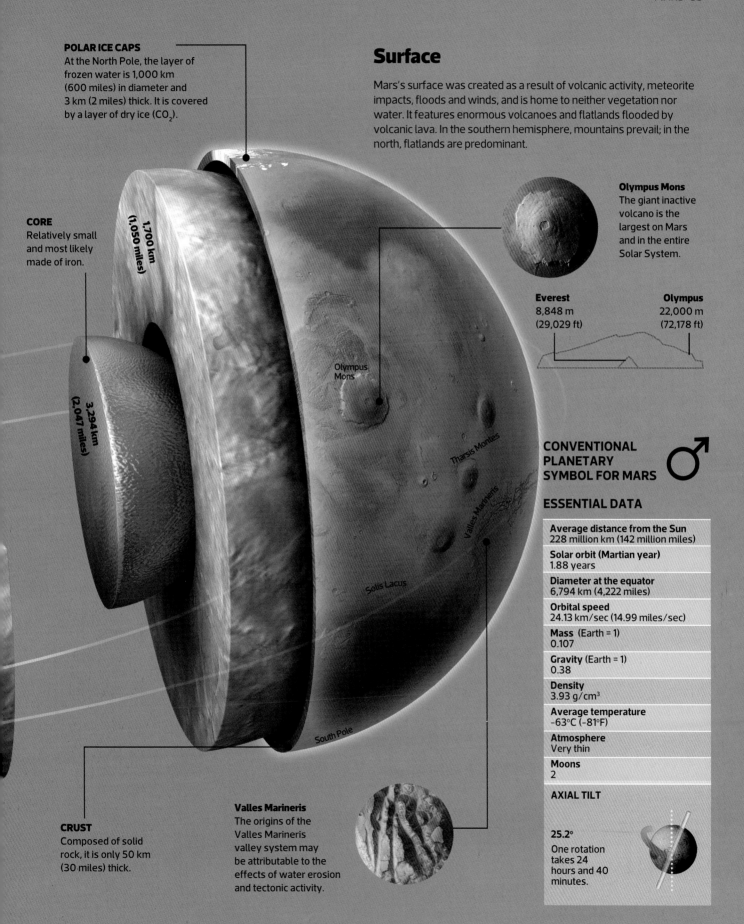

Surface

Mars's surface was created as a result of volcanic activity, meteorite impacts, floods and winds, and is home to neither vegetation nor water. It features enormous volcanoes and flatlands flooded by volcanic lava. In the southern hemisphere, mountains prevail; in the north, flatlands are predominant.

POLAR ICE CAPS
At the North Pole, the layer of frozen water is 1,000 km (600 miles) in diameter and 3 km (2 miles) thick. It is covered by a layer of dry ice (CO_2).

CORE
Relatively small and most likely made of iron.

1,700 km (1,050 miles)

3,294 km (2,047 miles)

Olympus Mons

Tharsis Montes

Valles Marineris

Solis Lacus

South Pole

Olympus Mons
The giant inactive volcano is the largest on Mars and in the entire Solar System.

Everest
8,848 m (29,029 ft)

Olympus
22,000 m (72,178 ft)

CONVENTIONAL PLANETARY SYMBOL FOR MARS ♂

ESSENTIAL DATA

Average distance from the Sun 228 million km (142 million miles)	
Solar orbit (Martian year) 1.88 years	
Diameter at the equator 6,794 km (4,222 miles)	
Orbital speed 24.13 km/sec (14.99 miles/sec)	
Mass (Earth = 1) 0.107	
Gravity (Earth = 1) 0.38	
Density 3.93 g/cm³	
Average temperature -63°C (-81°F)	
Atmosphere Very thin	
Moons 2	

AXIAL TILT

25.2°
One rotation takes 24 hours and 40 minutes.

CRUST
Composed of solid rock, it is only 50 km (30 miles) thick.

Valles Marineris
The origins of the Valles Marineris valley system may be attributable to the effects of water erosion and tectonic activity.

Jupiter

The largest planet in the Solar System. Its diameter is eleven times greater than Earth's, its mass is 300 times greater, and it spins at a speed of 40,000 km (24,850 miles) per hour. One of the most distinctive features of its atmosphere is the so-called 'Great Red Spot', an enormous area of high-pressure turbulence. The planet has several satellites and a fine ring of particles that orbit around it.

Composition

Jupiter is a huge mass of hydrogen and helium, compressed in liquid form. Little is known about its core, and it has not been possible to measure its size; however, it is believed to be a metallic solid with a high density.

CONVENTIONAL PLANETARY SYMBOL FOR JUPITER ♃

ESSENTIAL DATA

Average distance from the Sun 778 million km (483 million miles)	
Solar orbit (Jovian year) 11 years 312 days	
Diameter at the equator 142,800 km (88,730 miles)	
Orbital speed 13.07 km/sec (8.12 miles/sec)	
Mass (Earth = 1) 318	
Gravity (Earth = 1) 2.36	
Density 1.33 g/cm³	
Average temperature -120°C (-184°F)	
Atmosphere Very dense	
Moons 67	

AXIAL TILT

3.1°

One rotation takes 9 hours and 55 minutes.

CRUST
It is 1,000 km (620 miles) thick.

37,700 km (23,400 miles)

27,000 km (16,800 miles)

CORE

INNER MANTLE
Comprising metallic hydrogen, an element that can only be found at very high temperatures and pressures.

OUTER MANTLE
Comprising liquid hydrogen and helium. The outer mantle merges with the planet's atmosphere.

AMAZING FACT

So far, 67 moons have been discovered, plus an additional dozen 'temporary' moons whose nature and orbits have yet to be confirmed.

ATMOSPHERE
It encompasses the inner liquid and solid core layers.

89.8 per cent hydrogen

10.2 per cent helium with traces of methane and ammonia

Galilean moons

Of Jupiter's many moons, four can be seen from Earth with the use of binoculars. They are known as the Galilean moons, in honour of their discoverer, Galileo Galilei. Io is the most volcanically active world in our Solar System, and Europa may be home to an ocean beneath its ice crust.

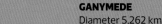

GANYMEDE
Diameter 5,262 km (3,270 miles)

EUROPA
Diameter 3,122 km (1,940 miles)

IO
Diameter 3,643 km (2,264 miles)

CALLISTO
Diameter 4,821 km (2,995 miles)

Winds

The planet's surface winds blow in opposite directions and in contiguous bands. Slight variations in their individual temperature and chemical composition are responsible for the colours of the bands. The hostile environment – winds can exceed 600 km/h (370 mph) – is capable of causing storms, such as the Great Red Spot. It is believed to consist mainly of ammonia gas and ice clouds.

RINGS
Formed by dust released by the planet's four inner moons.

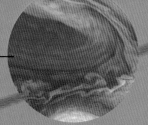

26,000 km
(16,150 miles)
is the length of the 'Great Red Spot'.

650,000,000 km
(404,000,000 miles)

Jupiter produces the largest planetary magnetosphere in the Solar System. It varies in size and shape depending on its interaction with solar wind (a continuous stream of plasma released by the Sun).

The magnetism of Jupiter

Jupiter's magnetic field is 20,000 times more intense than Earth's. The planet is surrounded by an enormous magnetic bubble – the magnetosphere. Its magnetotail extends beyond Saturn's orbit.

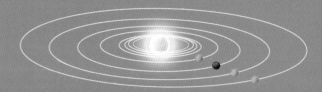

Saturn

Just like Jupiter, Saturn is a huge ball of gas that encompasses a small solid core. To an onlooker, it would seem like just another yellow-tinted star; however, with the help of a telescope, its rings can be clearly distinguished. Ten times farther from the Sun than Earth, it is the least dense of all the planets, and would even be able to float in the sea.

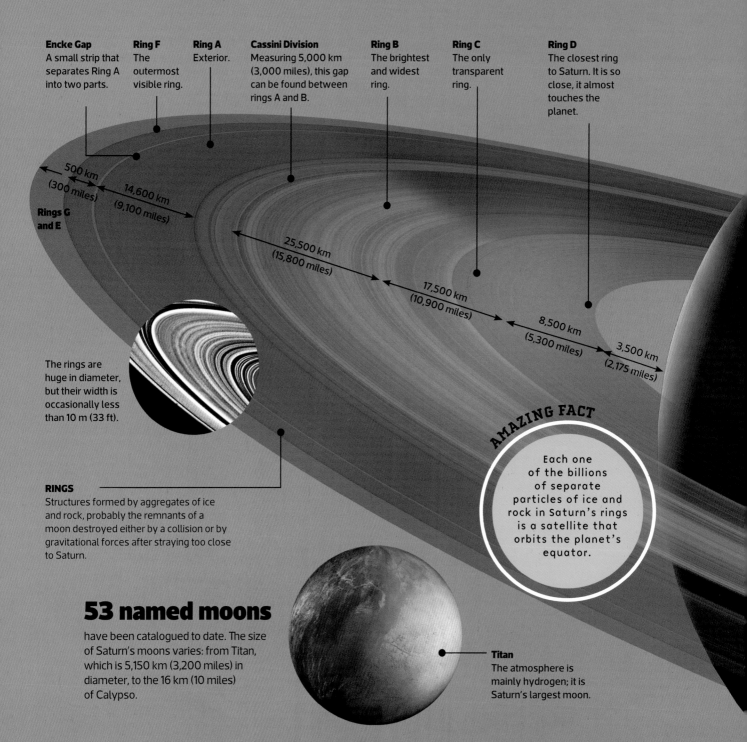

Encke Gap
A small strip that separates Ring A into two parts.

Ring F
The outermost visible ring.

Ring A
Exterior.

Cassini Division
Measuring 5,000 km (3,000 miles), this gap can be found between rings A and B.

Ring B
The brightest and widest ring.

Ring C
The only transparent ring.

Ring D
The closest ring to Saturn. It is so close, it almost touches the planet.

500 km
(300 miles)

14,600 km
(9,100 miles)

Rings G and E

25,500 km
(15,800 miles)

17,500 km
(10,900 miles)

8,500 km
(5,300 miles)

3,500 km
(2,175 miles)

The rings are huge in diameter, but their width is occasionally less than 10 m (33 ft).

RINGS
Structures formed by aggregates of ice and rock, probably the remnants of a moon destroyed either by a collision or by gravitational forces after straying too close to Saturn.

AMAZING FACT
Each one of the billions of separate particles of ice and rock in Saturn's rings is a satellite that orbits the planet's equator.

53 named moons

have been catalogued to date. The size of Saturn's moons varies: from Titan, which is 5,150 km (3,200 miles) in diameter, to the 16 km (10 miles) of Calypso.

Titan
The atmosphere is mainly hydrogen; it is Saturn's largest moon.

Surface

Saturn has a surface of clouds, which form bands attributable to the rotation of the planet on its axis. Saturn's clouds are calmer and less colourful than those of Jupiter. Temperatures in the highest (white) clouds reach -140°C (-220°F) and a layer of fog extends over them.

Fog

White clouds

Deep, orange clouds

Blue clouds

ATMOSPHERE
Mainly composed of hydrogen and helium. The remainder is made up of sulphurs (responsible for its yellowy tones), methane and other gases.

97 per cent hydrogen

2 per cent helium

1 per cent sulphurs and other gases

CONVENTIONAL PLANETARY SYMBOL FOR SATURN

ħ

ESSENTIAL DATA

Average distance from the Sun 1,427 million km (887 million miles)	
Solar orbit (Saturnian year) 29 years 154 days	
Diameter at the equator 120,600 km (74,940 miles)	
Orbital speed 9.66 km/sec (6 miles/sec)	
Mass (Earth = 1) 95	
Gravity (Earth = 1) 0.92	
Density 0.69 g/cm³	
Average temperature -125°C (-193°F)	
Atmosphere Very dense	
Named Moons 53	

AXIAL TILT

26.7°
One rotation takes 10 hours and 39 minutes.

Winds
Wind speeds of up to 360 km/h (225 mph) can be reached at the equator. The planet can experience torrid storms.

30,000 km (18,650 miles)

14,000 km (8,700 miles)

32,000 km (19,900 miles)

MANTLE
The planet is externally covered by a mantle of liquid hydrogen and helium that extends into its gaseous atmosphere.

HYDROGEN LAYER
Liquid hydrogen encompasses the outer core.

CORE
Comprising rock and metallic elements such as silicates and iron. On the inside, it is similar to Jupiter.

12,000°C (21,600°F)

is the core temperature.

OUTER CORE
Water, methane and ammonia encompass the hot rocky core.

Uranus

At first glance, Uranus seems like just another star at the farthest limits of the naked eye's reach. It is almost four times larger than Earth and is unique in that its rotation axis is tilted to almost 98 degrees relative to its orbital plain, meaning one of its poles is always facing the Sun. Uranus's orbit is so large that the planet takes 84 years to orbit the Sun just once.

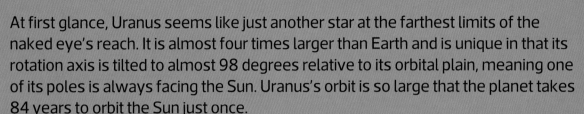

Magnetic field

Uranus's magnetic field is 50 times greater than Earth's and is tilted 60 degrees compared to its rotation axis. On Uranus, magnetism is generated by the mantle and not the core.

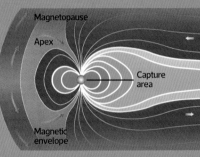

Magnetopause

Apex

Capture area

Magnetic envelope

Some scientists have suggested that Uranus's strange magnetic field may be attributable to the fact that there is no convection at its core because of cooling, or that it is magnetically inverted.

10,000°C
(18,000°F)

Core temperature

CONVENTIONAL PLANETARY SYMBOL FOR URANUS

ESSENTIAL DATA

Average distance from the Sun	2.87 billion km (1.78 billion miles)
Solar orbit (Uranian year)	84 years 36 days
Diameter at the equator	51,800 km (32,190 miles)
Orbital speed	6.82 km/sec (4.24 miles/sec)
Mass (Earth = 1)	14.5
Gravity (Earth = 1)	0.89
Density	1.32 g/cm³
Average temperature	–210°C (–346°F)
Atmosphere	Not dense
Moons	27

AXIAL TILT

97.9°
One rotation takes 17 hours and 14 minutes.

CORE
Comprising siliceous rocks and ice.

MANTLE 1
Comprising water, ice, methane gas, ammonia and ions.

MANTLE 2
Around the mantle, there may be another layer of liquid molecular hydrogen and liquid helium with a small amount of methane.

ATMOSPHERE
Comprising hydrogen, methane, helium and small amounts of acetylene and other hydrocarbons.

–210°C
(–346°F)

Average temperature.

10,000 km (6,000 miles)

17,000 km (10,500 miles)

10,000 km (6,000 miles)

85 per cent hydrogen

12 per cent helium

3 per cent methane

Nu and Mu
The planet's two outermost rings; their discovery was made public in 2005.

Epsilon

Lambda

Delta

Gamma

Eta

Beta

Alpha

4

5

6

1986U2R

Rings

Just like all the Solar System's giant planets, Uranus has a planetary ring system similar to that orbiting Saturn, but much darker. As a result, it is not possible to see the rings with any level of ease. The 13 rings that orbit the planet's equator were discovered in 1977. In 1986, they were explored by *Voyager 2*.

Satellites

Twenty-seven moons orbit the planet. The first two were discovered in 1787 and a further ten by the *Voyager 2* space probe in 1986. They were baptized in honour of characters in the works of William Shakespeare and Alexander Pope, a feature that makes them unique. Only a handful can be considered large, with most measuring just a few kilometres across.

MOONS
Uranus has small moons that are as black as oil, discovered by *Voyager 2*, in addition to the larger moons Miranda, Ariel, Umbriel, Oberon and Titania. The latter two measure over 1,500 km (900 miles) in diameter.

TITANIA
1,578 km
(981 miles)

UMBRIEL
1,170 km
(727 miles)

ARIEL
1,158 km
(720 miles)

MIRANDA
472 km
(293 miles)

OBERON
1,522 km
(946 miles)

RAY REFRACTION

1 On Uranus, sunlight is reflected by a curtain of clouds that sits beneath a layer of methane gas.

2 When the light reflection penetrates this layer, the methane gas absorbs the beams of red light and enables blue light to pass, which is responsible for the planet's blue-green tone.

Surface

For a long time, it was believed that Uranus's surface was smooth. However, the Hubble telescope showed that it is a dynamic planet with the brightest clouds in the Solar System, and with a weak planetary ring system that oscillates like an unbalanced wheel.

Atmosphere

Rays of sunlight

Uranus

Atmosphere

Rays of sunlight

Uranus

Neptune

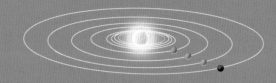

The Solar System's outermost gas planet is 30 times farther from the Sun than Earth, and looks like an extraordinary blue ball. This effect is attributed to the presence of methane in the outermost part of its atmosphere. Its moons, rings and incredible clouds all stand out, and its similarity to Uranus is also discernible. To scientists, Neptune is particularly special: its existence was proposed based on mathematical calculations and predictions.

Moons

Neptune has 14 natural satellites. Triton and Nereid, those farthest from the planet, were the first to be seen from Earth using a telescope. The remainder were observed from space by US spacecraft *Voyager 2*. All their names correspond to gods of the sea from Greek mythology.

89.8 per cent
hydrogen

10.2 per cent
helium

TRITON

Neptune's largest moon measures 2,706 km (1,681 miles) in diameter. At -235°C (-391°F) it is one of the Solar System's coldest bodies, and its surface is marked with dark grooves, formed by the dust precipitated following the eruptions of its geysers and volcanoes.

COMPOSITION

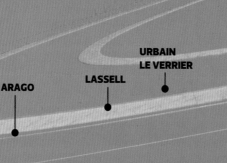

Neptune's rings are dark, although their composition is not known; it is also believed that they are not stable. For example, Liberty is the outermost part of the ring and it may completely vanish by the end of this century.

Rings

From Earth, they look like arcs. However, we now know that they are rings of dust that shine, reflecting rays of sunlight. Their names honour the first scientists to study the planet.

GALLE

URBAIN LE VERRIER

LASSELL

ARAGO

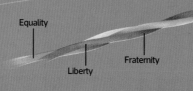

ADAMS
Located 63,000 km (39,000 miles) from the planet's core. It is a formation of three intertwining rings named Liberty, Fraternity and Equality.

Equality

Liberty

Fraternity

AMAZING FACT

Triton is the only large moon in the Solar System that orbits in the opposite direction to the rotation of its planet.

Surface

White methane clouds encompass the planet. The winds circulate from east to west, in the opposite direction to the planet's rotation, reaching speeds of 2,000 km/h (1,250 mph).

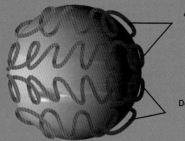

Ascending winds

Descending winds

GREAT DARK SPOT

A giant storm, the size of Earth and similar to the Great Red Spot on Jupiter, stood out against Neptune's surface. It was first seen in 1989 and broke up in 1994.

Structure

Neptune has a rocky silicate core, covered by a mantle of frozen water, ammonia, hydrogen and methane. The core and mantle occupy two-thirds of the planet's interior. The final third is the thick, dense atmosphere, which consists of a mixture of hot gases, comprising hydrogen, helium, water and methane.

7,200 km (4,500 miles)

14,000 km (8,700 miles)

6,000 km (3,750 miles)

CORE
The typical core of gas planets is repeated on Neptune – a rocky sphere that turns molten towards the surface.

MANTLE 1
The component materials of this layer convert from a solid to a gaseous state.

MANTLE 2
Containing a higher level of gaseous material than solid material.

ATMOSPHERE
The gases that make up the atmosphere are concentrated in bands similar to those found on other gas giants. They form a cloud system that is as active, or even more active, than the system on Jupiter.

CONVENTIONAL PLANETARY SYMBOL FOR NEPTUNE

♆

ESSENTIAL DATA

Average distance from the Sun	4.5 billion km (2.8 billion miles)
Solar orbit (Neptunian year)	164 years 264 days
Diameter at the equator	49,500 km (30,750 miles)
Orbital speed	5.48 km/sec (3.41 miles/sec)
Mass (Earth = 1)	17.2
Gravity (Earth = 1)	1.12
Density	1.64 g/cm³
Average temperature	–200°C (–382°F)
Atmosphere	Dense
Moons	14

AXIAL TILT

28.3°
One rotation takes 16 hours and 36 minutes.

Pluto

Until 2006, Pluto was considered the ninth planet in the Solar System. In that year, however, the International Astronomical Union (IAU) decided to designate it a 'dwarf planet'. Little is known about this tiny body in the Solar System. However, some of its characteristics make it particularly special: its unique orbit, its axial tilt, and the fact that it is an object belonging to the Kuiper Belt.

Charon

Charon is Pluto's largest satellite. Incredibly, the diameter of Pluto's biggest moon is almost half that of the planet itself. Its surface appears to be covered in ice, unlike Pluto, the surface of which consists of frozen nitrogen, methane and carbon dioxide. One theory is that Charon was formed from ice that was torn from Pluto by a collision with another object.

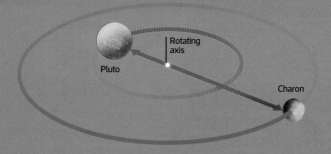

SYNCHRONIZED ORBITS
It is often considered that Pluto and Charon form a double planetary system. The rotation between the two bodies is unique: their sightline is never broken, and it appears as if they are united by an invisible bar. They are synchronized to such an extent that Charon can only ever be seen from one side of Pluto; from the other side the moon is never visible.

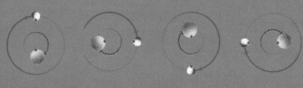

CONVENTIONAL PLANETARY SYMBOL FOR PLUTO ♇

ESSENTIAL DATA

Average distance from the Sun	5.9 billion km (3.7 billion miles)
Solar orbit (Plutonian year)	247.9 years
Diameter at the equator	2,247 km (1,396 miles)
Orbital speed	4.75 km/sec (2.95 miles/sec)
Mass (Earth = 1)	0.002
Gravity (Earth = 1)	0.062
Density	2.05 g/cm³
Average temperature	−230°C (−382°F)
Atmosphere	Very thin
Moons	5

AXIAL TILT

122°
One rotation takes 153 hours.

1,172 km
(728 miles)

is the diameter of Charon, half that of Pluto.

Other moons

Apart from Charon, discovered in 1978, Pluto has four other moons: Nix and Hydra, discovered in 2005 by the Hubble telescope, and two further moons (P4 and P5) that remain unnamed, discovered in 2011 and 2012.

DENSITY
The density of Charon is 1.678 g/cm³; it is therefore assumed that rocks do not represent a large part of its composition.

Surface

Little is known about Pluto. However, the Hubble telescope has shown that its surface is covered by a combination of frozen nitrogen and methane. The presence of methane in its solid state would suggest that the surface temperature is less than -203°C (-333°F). However, this depends on the point at which this 'dwarf planet' is in orbit, given that its distance from the Sun can range between 30 and 50 astronomical units.

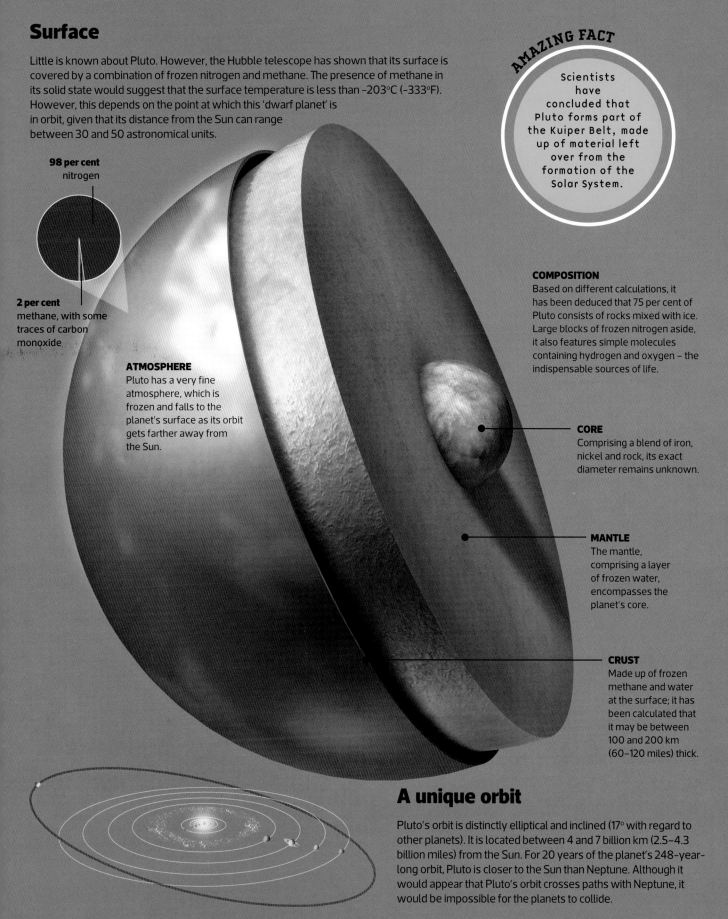

98 per cent
nitrogen

2 per cent
methane, with some traces of carbon monoxide

ATMOSPHERE
Pluto has a very fine atmosphere, which is frozen and falls to the planet's surface as its orbit gets farther away from the Sun.

COMPOSITION
Based on different calculations, it has been deduced that 75 per cent of Pluto consists of rocks mixed with ice. Large blocks of frozen nitrogen aside, it also features simple molecules containing hydrogen and oxygen – the indispensable sources of life.

CORE
Comprising a blend of iron, nickel and rock, its exact diameter remains unknown.

MANTLE
The mantle, comprising a layer of frozen water, encompasses the planet's core.

CRUST
Made up of frozen methane and water at the surface; it has been calculated that it may be between 100 and 200 km (60–120 miles) thick.

A unique orbit

Pluto's orbit is distinctly elliptical and inclined (17° with regard to other planets). It is located between 4 and 7 billion km (2.5–4.3 billion miles) from the Sun. For 20 years of the planet's 248-year-long orbit, Pluto is closer to the Sun than Neptune. Although it would appear that Pluto's orbit crosses paths with Neptune, it would be impossible for the planets to collide.

Asteroids and Meteors

Since the time the Solar System began to form, the fusion, collision and break-up of different materials has played an essential role in the formation of the planets. These 'small' rocks are remnants of this process. They are witnesses that provide data to help us understand the extraordinary phenomena that began 4.6 billion years ago. On Earth, these objects are associated with episodes that would later influence evolutionary processes.

The nature of meteorites

One of the main goals in the study of meteorites is to determine their make-up. They contain both extraterrestrial gases and solids. Scientific tests have made it possible to confirm that, in some cases, the objects came from the Moon or Mars. However, for the most part, meteorites are associated with asteroids.

HOW A METEORITE MAKES IMPACT
When penetrating Earth's atmosphere, meteorites do not completely vaporize – on reaching the ground they leave a footprint called a 'crater'. Furthermore, they contribute exotic rock material to Earth's surface, such as large amounts of iridium, an element that is scarce on Earth but common in the composition of meteorites.

10–70 km/sec
(6–43 km/sec)

is the impact speed of a meteorite hitting Earth.

TYPES OF METEORITES

Aerolites
Notable for their olivine and pyroxene content. This category subdivides into chondrites and nonchondrites.

Iron meteorites
Abundant in iron-nickel compounds. Generated during the break-up of asteroids.

Siderolites
Stony-iron meteorites composed of similar amounts of iron, nickel and silicates.

1 **EXPLOSION**
Friction with the air increases the temperature of the meteorite, until it starts to ignite, leading to the visible phenomenon known as a 'shooting star'.

2 **DIVISION**
Most meteorites disintegrate on entering the atmosphere and reach the Earth as small particles or dust.

3 **IMPACT**
On impact, the meteorite is compressed and carves out a dent, or crater, in Earth's surface.

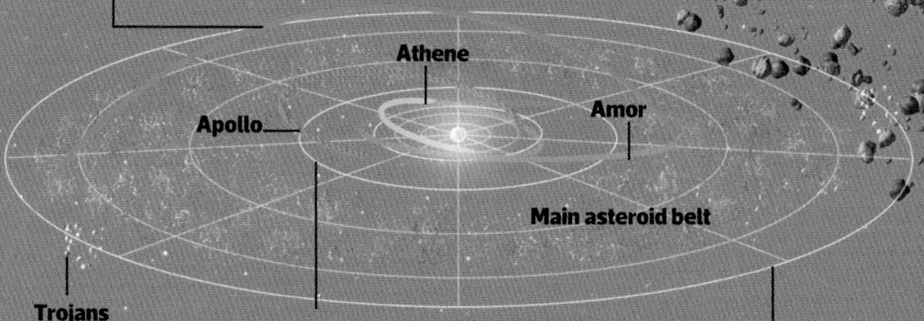

Hidalgo
Orbits the Sun once
every 14 years.

Athene

Apollo

Amor

Main asteroid belt

Trojans
They share their orbit
with Jupiter.

Mars's orbit

Jupiter's orbit

Asteroids

Fragments of rock and metal in a variety of shapes and sizes
orbit the Sun. Most, over a million, are located in the main asteroid
belt between the orbits of Mars and Jupiter. Others circle in orbits
close to Earth (the Amor, Apollo and Athene groups) or share their
orbit with Jupiter (the so-called Trojans). In reality, the asteroid
belt is not as densely packed as depicted.

TYPES OF ASTEROID
Despite the numerous
varieties of shapes and sizes,
three types of asteroid are
known. Depending on their
composition, they divide into
silicaceous, carbonaceous or
metallic asteroids.

IDA
An asteroid measuring
56 km (35 miles) long,
the surface of which is
scarred as a result of
collisions with other
bodies.

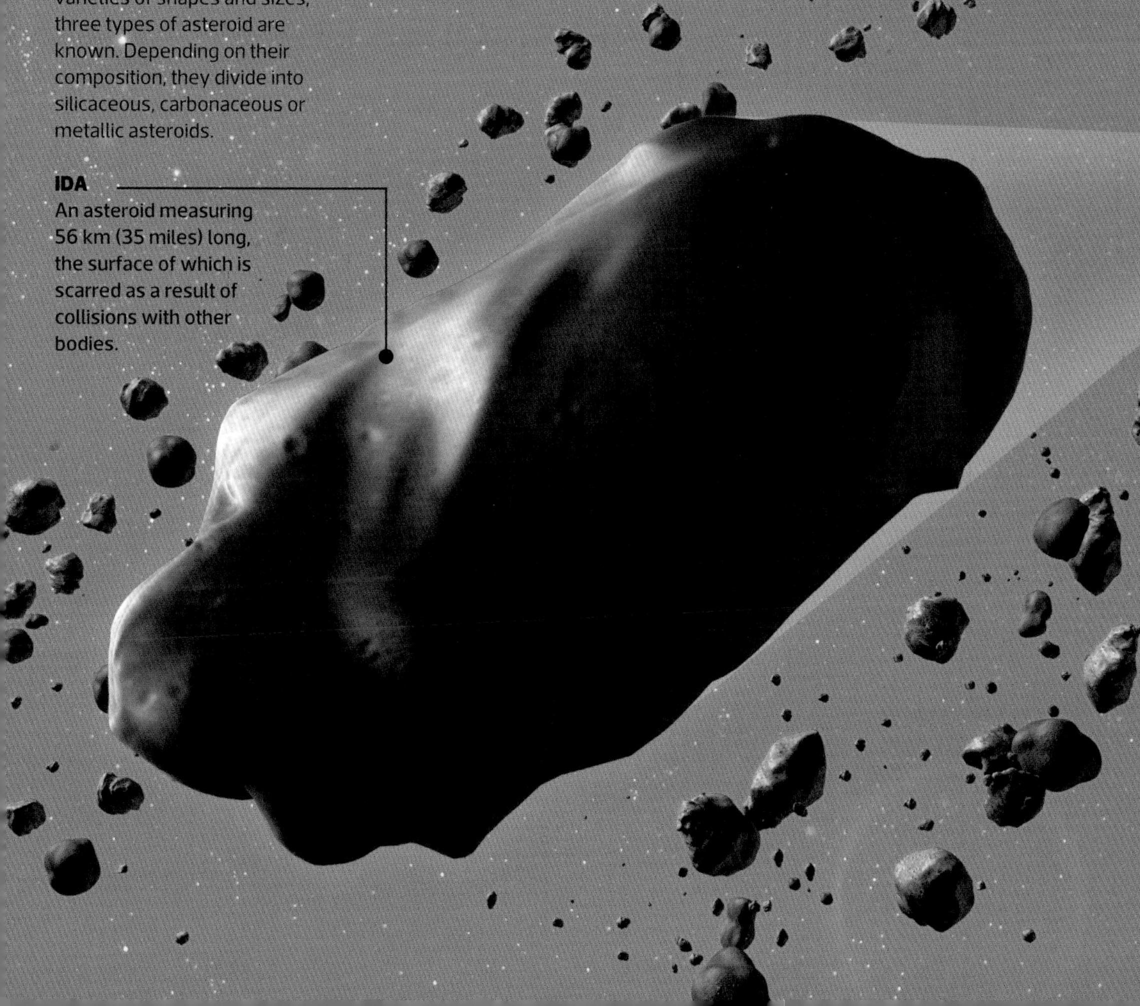

AMAZING FACT

A 17-m
(55-ft) wide
meteorite entered
Earth's atmosphere
on 15 February 2013,
and exploded over
Chelyabinsk, Russia,
in a 500-kiloton
fireball.

950 km
(590 miles)

is the diameter of
Ceres, the first asteroid
discovered and the
largest known.

Comets

Comets are small, irregularly shaped objects, measuring less than a few kilometres in diameter, that are usually frozen and dark in colour. They are made of dust, rock, gases and organic molecules rich in carbon, and can be found orbiting in the Kuiper Belt or the so-called Oort cloud. However, many deviate towards the inner part of the Solar System, assuming new paths. When they warm up, their ice formations sublimate, forming their heads and long tails of gas and dust.

Deep Impact space mission

On 12 January 2005, as part of the Discovery Programme, the US Space Agency launched *Deep Impact*. This spacecraft was designed to launch a projectile that impacted against the comet 9P/Tempel to obtain samples to be studied on Earth.

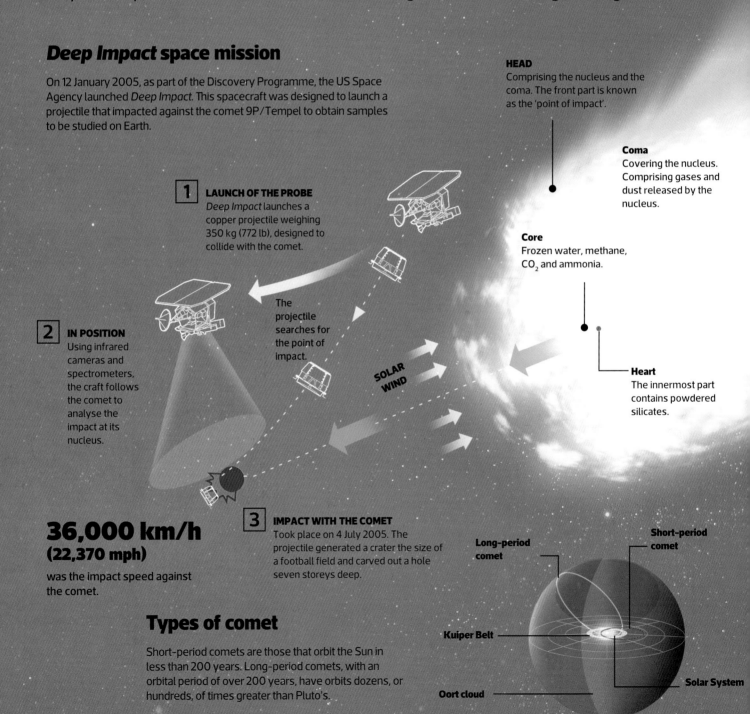

1 LAUNCH OF THE PROBE
Deep Impact launches a copper projectile weighing 350 kg (772 lb), designed to collide with the comet.

The projectile searches for the point of impact.

2 IN POSITION
Using infrared cameras and spectrometers, the craft follows the comet to analyse the impact at its nucleus.

SOLAR WIND

3 IMPACT WITH THE COMET
Took place on 4 July 2005. The projectile generated a crater the size of a football field and carved out a hole seven storeys deep.

36,000 km/h
(22,370 mph)

was the impact speed against the comet.

HEAD
Comprising the nucleus and the coma. The front part is known as the 'point of impact'.

Coma
Covering the nucleus. Comprising gases and dust released by the nucleus.

Core
Frozen water, methane, CO_2 and ammonia.

Heart
The innermost part contains powdered silicates.

Types of comet

Short-period comets are those that orbit the Sun in less than 200 years. Long-period comets, with an orbital period of over 200 years, have orbits dozens, or hundreds, of times greater than Pluto's.

Long-period comet

Short-period comet

Kuiper Belt

Oort cloud

Solar System

AMAZING FACT

Halley's Comet takes approximately 76 years to complete its orbit around the Sun, so it will next be visible from Earth in 2061.

HEAD

TAIL

ENVELOPE
Layers of hydrogen that are capable of forming a third tail.

TAIL OF DUST
Suspended dust particles form a wake that reflects sunlight, making the comet's tail luminous.

TAIL OF IONS
The tail of suspended gases generates a low intensity, luminous blue-coloured area. Gas molecules lose an electron and acquire an electrical charge.

FORMATION OF THE TAIL
Due to the effects of solar winds, when the comet gets closer to the Sun, the gases released travel farther away. Meanwhile, the dust particles form a wake that is curved, as it is less sensitive to the effects of solar winds. As the comet travels farther from the confines of the Solar System, the particles merge back together, and the tail disappears as the nucleus cools down and stops releasing gas.

Close to the Sun, the tail gets longer.

Moving away from the Sun, the tail disappears.

Sun

Earth

Mars

Jupiter

THE COMET'S ORBIT

The Moon and the Tides

It is believed that the Moon was created when a Mars-sized body crashed into Earth while it was still in formation. The expelled material scattered around Earth and, over time, it joined together to form the Moon. It is our planet's only natural satellite, and its gravitational pull influences the tides on Earth. The Moon's influence on bodies of water varies depending on its position.

Lunar movements

For each terrestrial orbit, the Moon spins on its own axis. As a result, the same side always faces Earth.

Lunar month
It takes 29.53 days to complete its phase.

Sidereal month
It takes 27.32 days to orbit Earth.

Hidden face
It was not until 1959, when the *Luna 3* probe photographed it, that the Moon's hidden face was seen for the first time.

Moon

Earth

Visible face

Lunar orbit

Aristarchus
is the brightest point on the Moon.

Oceanus Procellarum
is the biggest sea.

AMAZING FACT

The far side of the Moon is covered in craters and has only a few small lava seas. It looks very different from the side we can see from Earth.

The tides

The body of water closest to the Moon feels its gravitational pull more strongly, while the opposite side of Earth is less affected. Nonetheless, the Sun's pull also influences the movement of the tides. When the tide rises, it is known as high tide; when it lowers, low tide.

1 **NEW MOON**
Spring tide
As the Sun and Moon are aligned, they result in the highest high tides and the lowest low tides.

2 **FIRST QUARTER**
Neap tide
In a right angle with the Earth, the Moon and the Sun generate the lowest high tides and the highest low tides.

3 **FULL MOON**
Spring tide
The Sun and Moon align once again, and the Sun counteracts the pull of the Moon.

4 **LAST QUARTER**
Neap tide
The Sun and Moon form a right angle again, causing the second neap tide.

KEY

Gravitational pull of the Moon.

Gravitational pull of the Sun.

Influence on the sea caused by the gravitational pull of the Moon.

Influence on the sea caused by the gravitational pull of the Sun.

The surface of the Moon

Ancient astronomers deduced that the dark patches on the Moon that can be seen with the naked eye were *maria* (seas). These dark areas contrast with the light areas (highlands with a higher number of craters).

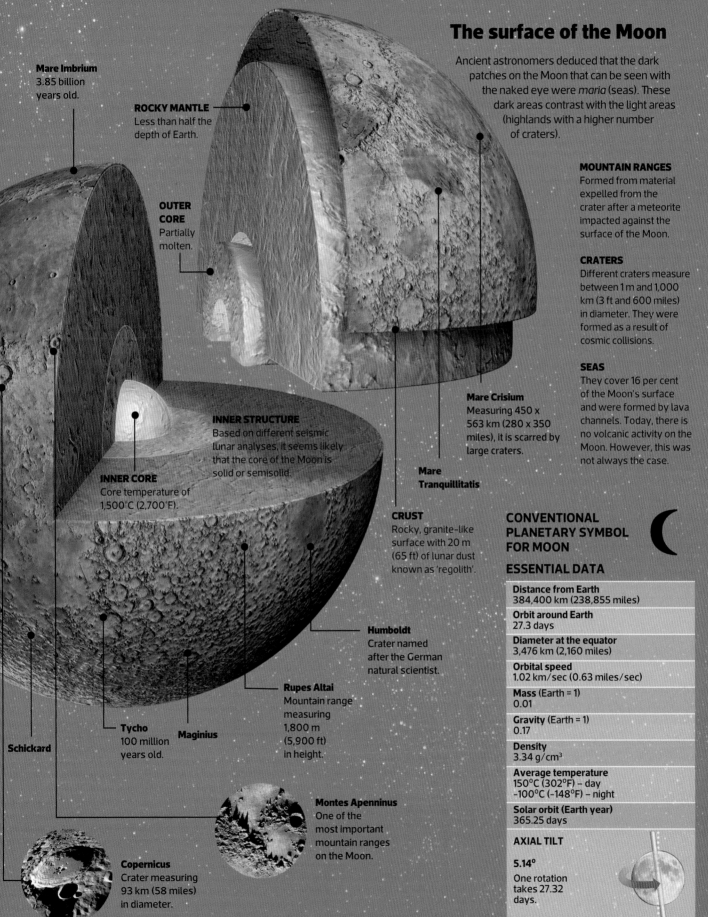

Mare Imbrium
3.85 billion years old.

ROCKY MANTLE
Less than half the depth of Earth.

OUTER CORE
Partially molten.

INNER STRUCTURE
Based on different seismic lunar analyses, it seems likely that the core of the Moon is solid or semisolid.

INNER CORE
Core temperature of 1,500˚C (2,700˚F).

Schickard

Tycho
100 million years old.

Maginius

Copernicus
Crater measuring 93 km (58 miles) in diameter.

Montes Apenninus
One of the most important mountain ranges on the Moon.

Rupes Altai
Mountain range measuring 1,800 m (5,900 ft) in height.

Humboldt
Crater named after the German natural scientist.

CRUST
Rocky, granite-like surface with 20 m (65 ft) of lunar dust known as 'regolith'.

Mare Tranquillitatis

Mare Crisium
Measuring 450 x 563 km (280 x 350 miles), it is scarred by large craters.

MOUNTAIN RANGES
Formed from material expelled from the crater after a meteorite impacted against the surface of the Moon.

CRATERS
Different craters measure between 1 m and 1,000 km (3 ft and 600 miles) in diameter. They were formed as a result of cosmic collisions.

SEAS
They cover 16 per cent of the Moon's surface and were formed by lava channels. Today, there is no volcanic activity on the Moon. However, this was not always the case.

CONVENTIONAL PLANETARY SYMBOL FOR MOON

ESSENTIAL DATA

Distance from Earth	384,400 km (238,855 miles)
Orbit around Earth	27.3 days
Diameter at the equator	3,476 km (2,160 miles)
Orbital speed	1.02 km/sec (0.63 miles/sec)
Mass (Earth = 1)	0.01
Gravity (Earth = 1)	0.17
Density	3.34 g/cm³
Average temperature	150°C (302°F) – day −100°C (−148°F) – night
Solar orbit (Earth year)	365.25 days

AXIAL TILT

5.14°
One rotation takes 27.32 days.

Eclipses

At least four times a year, the centres of the Moon, the Sun and the Earth fully align, resulting in one of the most attractive astronomical events to the casual observer: an eclipse. Solar eclipses also provide astronomers with an amazing opportunity for scientific investigation.

Total lunar eclipse seen from Earth
The orange colour is attributable to the refracted rays of sunlight, which are discoloured by the Earth's atmosphere.

Annular solar eclipse seen from Earth

Solar eclipse

When the Moon passes between Earth and the Sun, it projects a shadow on a given part of Earth's surface, creating a shadow zone and a penumbra zone. Spectators in the shadow zone will see the Moon fully block the Sun; such an event is known as a total solar eclipse. Spectators in the penumbra zone will see a partial solar eclipse.

During solar eclipses, astronomers take advantage of the shadow cast over the Sun to study its atmosphere using special equipment.

ALIGNMENT

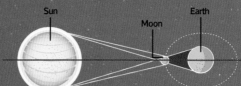

Sun

Moon

Earth

Watching a solar eclipse
A solar eclipse should never be viewed with the naked eye, as it can burn the retina. Special glasses must be used.

Black polymer filter with an optical density of 5.0. This prevents the retina suffering burn damage and offers a clear view of the Sun.

TYPES OF SOLAR ECLIPSES

Total
The Moon is positioned between the Sun and Earth, within the shadow zone.

Annular
The diameter of the Moon is smaller than that of the Sun, and part of the Sun can be seen.

Partial
The Moon does not fully cover the Sun, which appears as a crescent.

SOLAR LIGHT

7.5 minutes

is the maximum duration of a solar eclipse.

Lunar eclipse

When Earth passes between the Moon and the Sun, the resulting phenomenon is a lunar eclipse, which may be total, partial or penumbral. A totally eclipsed Moon takes on a characteristic reddish colour, as the light is refracted by the Earth's atmosphere. When part of the Moon is within the shadow zone, and the rest within the penumbral zone, the result is a partial eclipse.

107 minutes

is the maximum duration of a lunar eclipse.

ALIGNMENT

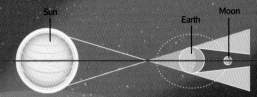

Sun   Earth   Moon

During an eclipse, the Moon is not completely black: it assumes a reddish colour.

FULL MOON
TOTAL ECLIPSE

Shadow zone

PARTIAL
ECLIPSE

Lunar orbit

PENUMBRAL
ECLIPSE

Shadow zone

Penumbral
zone

NEW MOON
TOTAL ECLIPSE

EARTH

Penumbral
zone

Earth's orbit

TYPES OF LUNAR ECLIPSES

Total
The Moon is completely within the shadow zone.

Partial
The Moon is only partially within the shadow zone.

Penumbral
The Moon is within the penumbral zone.

CYCLE OF ECLIPSES

Eclipses are repeated every 223 lunar months, or every 18 years and 11 days. These periods are called 'saros'.

ECLIPSES IN A YEAR

2 MINIMUM

7 MAXIMUM

4 AVERAGE

ECLIPSES IN ONE SAROS

41 SOLAR ECLIPSES

29 LUNAR ECLIPSES

70 TOTAL

Space Exploration

The space age began in 1957 with the launch of the first artificial satellite. Today, advances in astronautics have helped develop the autonomous navigation system, by which a ship may orbit a planet by itself. An example is the *Mars Express*, launched in 2003 and powered exclusively by solar energy. It explored a number of objectives and took pictures of Mars.

Auto Navigation System

Unmanned spacecraft, such as satellites orbiting planets, transmit their data back to Earth via radio equipment whose coverage depends on their type of orbit Probes are used to land on the surface, as has been done on Venus, Mars and the Moon. The real work begins when the unit reaches its target. The instruments are activated and collect data that are sent to Earth for analysis.

Solar panel
Provides energy for navigation.

Fuel tanks
Hold 267 litres (70 gallons) of propellant each.

Thrusters
Used to correct the orbit.

CONVENTIONAL NAVIGATION
During the rendezvous, optical navigation based on Earth is limited by the time the light takes to make the return trip to the ship.

Navigation systems based on Earth require radio tracking.

The pictures taken are transmitted to Earth and navigation commands are sent to the spacecraft.

2 The probe deployed its solar panels and began a life of its own, using solar energy. It sent signals to Earth to check the correct operation of the instruments.

LAUNCH

LAUNCH

The manoeuvres are calculated in the ground station and the parameters are transmitted to the spacecraft.

1 On 2 June 2003, *Mars Express* took off with a *Soyuz* rocket from Kazakhstan. Once it had escaped Earth's orbit, the probe separated from its thrusters and began its path to Mars's orbit.

4 Data transmission to Earth occurs when the probe is at the maximum height of its orbit around Mars. At that time, it stops pointing towards the red planet and directs its high-gain antenna towards Earth. *Mars Express* began orbiting Mars in December 2003 and continues today.

High-gain antenna
To communicate with Earth when it is farther away.

3 *Mars Express* started its journey to Mars, which would last almost seven months. From Darmstadt, Germany, its activity was monitored in the mission's control centre, which established radio communication with the probe.

Space programmes

Space probes are automatic vehicles. Some just pass by the planet they are studying at some distance, while others (orbiters) are placed in planetary orbit, from where they can send out smaller probes to land. Manned spacecraft, on the other hand, demand design conditions related to survival, navigation, control and transmission.

SPACEWALK
To collect more information, astronauts perform spacewalks outside the ship.

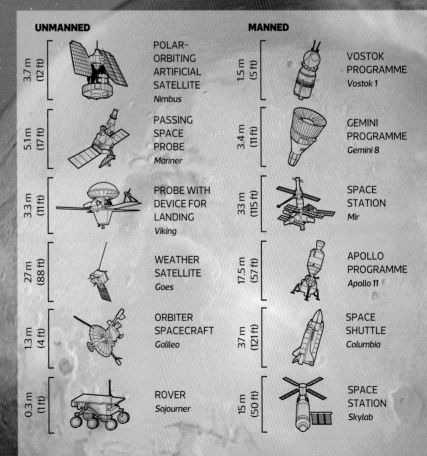

UNMANNED		MANNED	
3.7 m (12 ft)	POLAR-ORBITING ARTIFICIAL SATELLITE *Nimbus*	1.5 m (5 ft)	VOSTOK PROGRAMME *Vostok 1*
5.1 m (17 ft)	PASSING SPACE PROBE *Mariner*	3.4 m (11 ft)	GEMINI PROGRAMME *Gemini 8*
3.3 m (11 ft)	PROBE WITH DEVICE FOR LANDING *Viking*	33 m (115 ft)	SPACE STATION *Mir*
27 m (88 ft)	WEATHER SATELLITE *Goes*	17.5 m (57 ft)	APOLLO PROGRAMME *Apollo 11*
1.3 m (4 ft)	ORBITER SPACECRAFT *Galileo*	37 m (121 ft)	SPACE SHUTTLE *Columbia*
0.3 m (1 ft)	ROVER *Sojourner*	15 m (50 ft)	SPACE STATION *Skylab*

The Space Race

Astronautics came about in the late nineteenth century, when the Russian Konstantin Tsiolkovsky (1857–1935) foresaw the ability of a rocket to overcome the force of gravity. But the space race, the rivalry between world powers to conquer space, officially began in 1957 with the launch of the first Soviet artificial satellite, *Sputnik I*.

Sputnik I

It consisted of an aluminium sphere 58 cm (2 ft) in diameter, and for 21 days sent information on cosmic radiation, meteorites and the density and temperature of the Earth's upper atmosphere. It was destroyed by aerodynamic drag upon entering the atmosphere 57 days later.

THE FIRST
In 1917 in Germany, Romanian Hermann Oberth (1894–1989) suggested a liquid-fuelled rocket, which promoted the idea of spaceflight.

THE SECOND
American Robert Goddard (1882–1945) designed a rocket 3 m (10 ft) high. On ignition, it rose to 12 m (39 ft) and then crashed 56 m (184 ft) away.

THE THIRD
German physicist Wernher von Braun (1912–77), created the *Saturn V* rocket for NASA: the rocket that took men to the Moon in 1969 and 1972.

TECHNICAL DATA SHEET

Launch	October 1957
Orbital altitude	600 km (373 miles)
Orbital period	97 minutes
Weight	83.6 kg (184 lb)
Country	USSR

Antennae
Sputnik I had four antennae of between 2.4 and 2.9 m (8–9.5 ft) in length.

1609
GALILEO
Built the first astronomical telescope and observed lunar craters.

1798
CAVENDISH
Showed that the law of gravity is true for any pair of bodies.

1806
ROCKETS
The British Royal Navy used rockets as military weapons.

1838
DISTANCE
The distance to the star 61 Cygni, taking Earth's orbit as a reference, was measured.

1926
FIRST ROCKET
Robert Goddard launched the first liquid-fuelled rocket.

Sputnik II

It was the second satellite launched into Earth orbit by the Russians, and the first to carry a living being on board: the dog Laika. The dog was connected to a machine that recorded its vital signs, and an air-regeneration system provided it with oxygen.

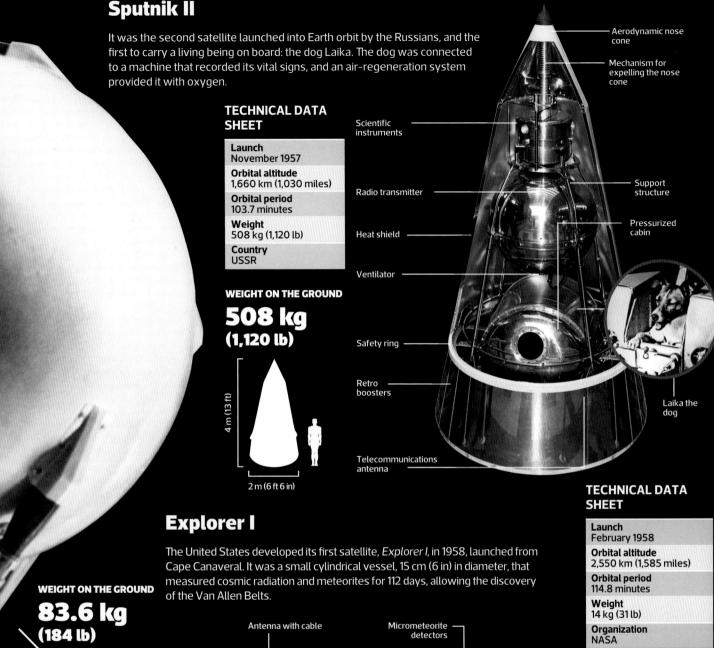

TECHNICAL DATA SHEET

Launch	November 1957
Orbital altitude	1,660 km (1,030 miles)
Orbital period	103.7 minutes
Weight	508 kg (1,120 lb)
Country	USSR

WEIGHT ON THE GROUND

508 kg
(1,120 lb)

4 m (13 ft)

2 m (6 ft 6 in)

Aerodynamic nose cone

Mechanism for expelling the nose cone

Scientific instruments

Radio transmitter

Heat shield

Ventilator

Support structure

Pressurized cabin

Safety ring

Retro boosters

Telecommunications antenna

Laika the dog

Explorer I

The United States developed its first satellite, *Explorer I*, in 1958, launched from Cape Canaveral. It was a small cylindrical vessel, 15 cm (6 in) in diameter, that measured cosmic radiation and meteorites for 112 days, allowing the discovery of the Van Allen Belts.

WEIGHT ON THE GROUND

83.6 kg
(184 lb)

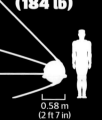

0.58 m (2 ft 7 in)

Antenna with cable

Micrometeorite detectors

Nose cone

Long-range transmitter

Internal temperature indicator

Fibreglass ring

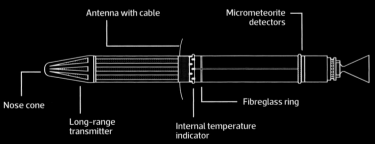

TECHNICAL DATA SHEET

Launch	February 1958
Orbital altitude	2,550 km (1,585 miles)
Orbital period	114.8 minutes
Weight	14 kg (31 lb)
Organization	NASA

WEIGHT ON THE GROUND

14 kg
(31 lb)

0.8 m (2 ft)

1927
SPACE SOCIETY
The Society for Space Travel was founded on 5 July in Germany.

1932
VON BRAUN
He began his research on rockets for the German Army.

1947
ROCKET PLANE
Chuck Yeager broke the sound barrier aboard the X-1 rocket plane.

1949
BUMPER
First two-stage rocket, which reached an altitude of 393 km (244 miles).

1957
SPUTNIK I
On 4 October, the Soviet Union launched the first satellite into space.

NASA

The National Aeronautics and Space Administration (NASA) is the US space agency. It was created in 1958 as part of the 'space race' being contested with the then Soviet Union, and it scheduled all national activities related to space exploration. NASA has a launch centre (Kennedy Space Center) and several facilities throughout the country.

NASA bases

NASA has facilities throughout the United States, which develop research, flight simulation and astronaut training. NASA headquarters are in Washington DC, and the Mission Control Center is in Houston, which is one of the locations where the Deep Space Network operates. This is a communications system with three locations in the world: Houston, Madrid and Canberra, which can capture signals in all directions and covers 100 per cent of the Earth's surface.

SHUTTLE LANDING FACILITY

Indian River

AMES RESEARCH CENTER
Founded in 1939, it is the experimental base for many missions. It is equipped with simulators and advanced technology.

JOHNSON SPACE CENTER
The control centre at Houston selects and trains astronauts and controls the take-off and landing of flights.

MARSHALL SPACE FLIGHT CENTER
Handles equipment transportation and propulsion systems, and was the lead centre for the space shuttle launch operations.

Visitor Complex

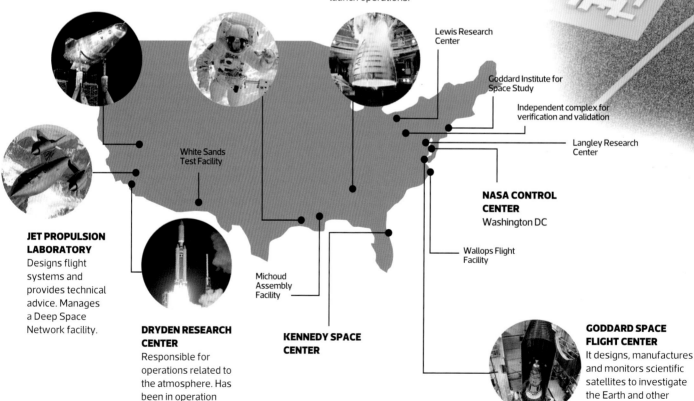

Lewis Research Center

Goddard Institute for Space Study

Independent complex for verification and validation

Langley Research Center

White Sands Test Facility

NASA CONTROL CENTER
Washington DC

Wallops Flight Facility

JET PROPULSION LABORATORY
Designs flight systems and provides technical advice. Manages a Deep Space Network facility.

DRYDEN RESEARCH CENTER
Responsible for operations related to the atmosphere. Has been in operation since 1947.

Michoud Assembly Facility

KENNEDY SPACE CENTER

GODDARD SPACE FLIGHT CENTER
It designs, manufactures and monitors scientific satellites to investigate the Earth and other planets.

Kennedy Space Center (KSC)

The KSC is located on Merritt Island, near Cape Canaveral, Florida. It measures 54 km (33 miles) long, covers an area of 352 km^2 (136 sq miles) and employs almost 17,000 people. It was established as the launch centre on 1 July 1962. KSC launched the *Apollo 11* mission that led to man walking on the Moon. It also hosted the take-off and landing of the space shuttle.

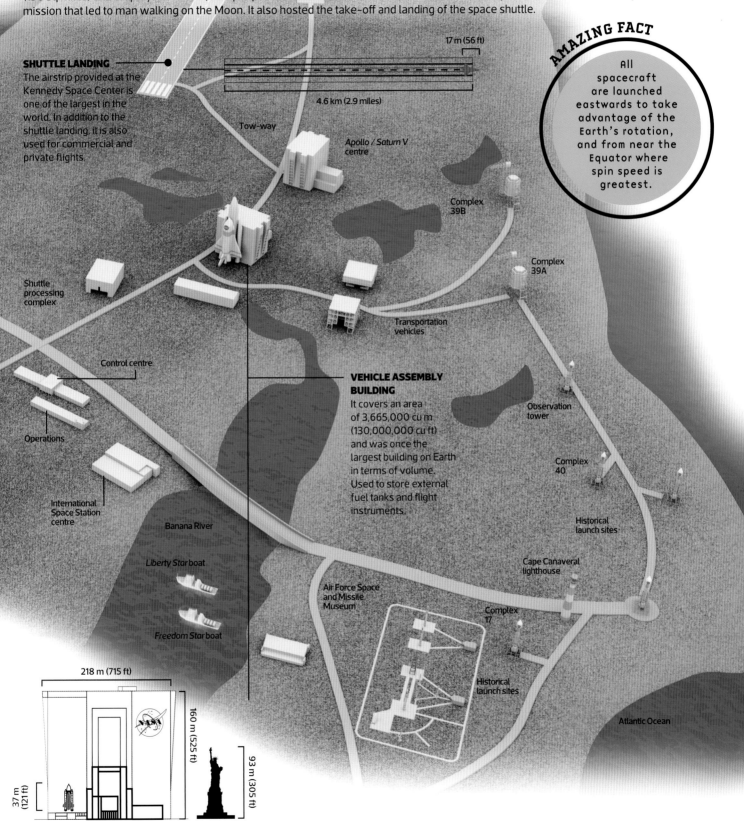

AMAZING FACT

All spacecraft are launched eastwards to take advantage of the Earth's rotation, and from near the Equator where spin speed is greatest.

17 m (56 ft)

4.6 km (2.9 miles)

SHUTTLE LANDING
The airstrip provided at the Kennedy Space Center is one of the largest in the world. In addition to the shuttle landing, it is also used for commercial and private flights.

Tow-way

Apollo / Saturn V centre

Complex 39B

Complex 39A

Shuttle processing complex

Transportation vehicles

Control centre

Operations

VEHICLE ASSEMBLY BUILDING
It covers an area of 3,665,000 cu m (130,000,000 cu ft) and was once the largest building on Earth in terms of volume. Used to store external fuel tanks and flight instruments.

Observation tower

Complex 40

International Space Station centre

Historical launch sites

Banana River

Liberty Star boat

Cape Canaveral lighthouse

Air Force Space and Missile Museum

Complex 17

Freedom Star boat

Historical launch sites

Atlantic Ocean

218 m (715 ft)

160 m (525 ft)

93 m (305 ft)

37 m (121 ft)

Other Space Agencies

Activity for exploration of the cosmos expanded in 1975, when the European Space Agency (ESA) was created. This intergovernmental organization has the largest investment budget after NASA. The *Mir* station, launched by the Russian Federal Space Agency (RKA), was 15 years in orbit and was a vital milestone for life in space. Other, younger agencies are Canada's CSA and Japan's JAXA.

Europe in space

The ESA was established as an organization in 1975, when the European Space Research Organization (ESRO) was merged with the European Launch Development Organization (ELDO). It has conducted missions of considerable importance, such as *Venus Express*, *Mars Express* and the *Ulysses* probe, the latter in conjunction with NASA.

EUROPEAN SPACE AGENCY

Founded	1975
Members	20
Annual budget	4 billion euros
Employees	2,200

AMAZING FACT

China's National Space Administration, established in 1993, landed its lunar rover *Chang'e 3* on the Moon on 14 December 2013.

EUROPEAN LAUNCH BASE

Latitude: 5° North, 500 km (311 miles) north of the Equator.
Being so near the Equator makes it easier to launch rockets into high orbits. The area is almost uninhabited and free of earthquakes.

KOUROU, FRENCH GUIANA

Area	850 km² (328 sq miles)
Total cost	1.6 billion euros
First operation	1968 (as a French base)
Employees	600

THE *ARIANE* FAMILY

The development of the *Ariane* rocket has led the ESA to become the market leader in launches. *Ariane* is chosen by Japanese, Canadian and American manufacturers.

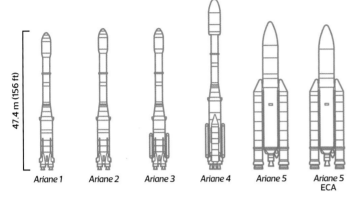

47.4 m (156 ft)

Ariane 1   Ariane 2   Ariane 3   Ariane 4   Ariane 5   Ariane 5 ECA

Over 200

Ariane rocket launches have been made by the ESA so far.

Springboard
After covering 3 km (1.9 miles) at 3.5 km/h (2.2 mph), the *Ariane* is ready for take-off.

Transportation route

Assembly building
Once assembly is completed, the rocket is transferred to the platform.

Towards the final design
The rocket is directed to the integration building to finalize details.

Canadian Space Agency

The CSA was established in 1990, although Canada had already developed some astronautical activities before that. The first Canadian launch was in 1962 with the satellite *Alouette I*. The CSA's most important project is its Earth observation satellite: *Radarsat–2*, launched in 2007, provides information on the environment and is used in cartography, hydrology, oceanography and agriculture.

Russian Federal Space Agency

The new agency was formed after the dissolution of the Soviet Union, and inherited its technology and launch sites. It was responsible for the orbiting *Mir* station, the forerunner to the International Space Station (ISS). *Mir* was assembled in orbit by launching different modules separately, between 1986 and 1996. It was destroyed in a controlled manner on 23 March 2001.

РОСКОСМОС

Mir station
Mir housed both cosmonauts (Russia) and astronauts (United States) in space.

Progress-M
Device for supplying food and fuel.

Solar panels
They provide power for the station.

Main module
For housing and overall control of the station.

Soyuz Rocket
Belonging to the Russian agency, it is used to launch a spacecraft into orbit.

Japanese Space Agency

On 1 October 2003, three independent organizations were merged to form JAXA: the Institute of Space and Aeronautical Science (ISSAS), the National Aerospace Laboratory (NAL) and the National Space Development Agency (NASDA). The highlight so far has been the *Hayabusa* mission, launched in May 2003. In November 2005, it became the first mission to land on an asteroid – Itokawa.

Man on the Moon

The space race culminated in President Kennedy's words that pledged a lunar landing before the end of the 1960s and the subsequent successful arrival on the Moon. For the first time in history a man could walk on the Moon's surface, in a mission which, including both the journey and the landing, lasted one week. It was the first journey that used two propulsion systems: one for take-off from Earth and another to return from the Moon to Earth.

TAKE-OFF

The module was powered by the *Saturn V* rocket, the heaviest ever built: almost 3,000 tons.

1 In 2 minutes 42 seconds, the rocket reached a speed of 9,800 km/h (6,090 mph) and entered Earth's orbit.

Launch platform

Stage 1

Gyro

Stage 3

Linked modules

2 The second stage ignited and the ship reached 23,000 km/h (14,290 mph).

3 The orbital and lunar modules stayed together until the trajectory correction.

4 After reaching lunar orbit, the *Eagle* module separated and prepared its landing.

EAGLE LUNAR MODULE

It was divided into two parts, one for ascent and another for descent. It docked with the orbital module for the ascent and the descent.

The voyage

The overall mission lasted about 200 hours. Two modules were used for the trip: one orbital (*Columbia*) and the other, the lunar module (*Eagle*). Both were attached to the *Saturn V* rocket until just after the third stage. After reaching lunar orbit, the *Eagle* module separated, with two astronauts on board, and prepared the landing. The return took place on 24 July. The stay on the Moon lasted 21 hours 38 minutes.

110 m (360 ft)

Saturn V
The rocket was as high as a 20-storey building.

Correction

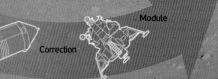
Module

RADAR ANTENNA FOR COUPLING

CABIN

DRIVE CONTROL ASSEMBLY

EXIT PLATFORM

OXYGENATOR TANK

EQUIPMENT FOR EXPERIMENTS

LM-5 *EAGLE*

Moon landing	20 July 1969
Height	6.5 m (21 ft)
Cabin volume	6.65 m³ (235 cu ft)
Crew	2
Organization	NASA

AMAZING FACT

AMAZING FACT

During the first landing, NASA limited Neil Armstrong's walk on the Moon to a maximum of 60 m (196 ft) away from the lunar module.

***COLUMBIA* ORBITAL MODULE**
Divided into two modules, allowing the presence of three crew in the cockpit.

MANOEUVRABLE ANTENNA

GASEOUS OXYGEN TANKS

VERY HIGH FREQUENCY ANTENNA

FUEL TANK

UNDERCARRIAGE

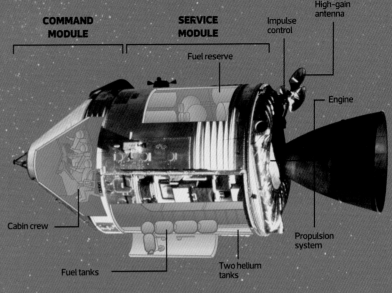

COMMAND MODULE
SERVICE MODULE
High-gain antenna
Impulse control
Fuel reserve
Engine
Cabin crew
Propulsion system
Fuel tanks
Two helium tanks

CSM-107 *COLUMBIA*

Launch	16 July 1969
Height	11 m (36 ft)
Diameter	3.9 m (13 ft)
Cabin volume	6.2 m³ (219 cu ft)
Crew	3
Organization	NASA

11 m (36 ft)

The crew

The three crew members had participated in the *Gemini* project, which was a very important preparation for the landing and moonwalks. Armstrong and Aldrin were the first humans to set foot on Earth's only satellite, while Collins orbited around the Moon at an altitude of 111 km (69 miles).

The huge *Eagle*
The astronauts reached only a little more than halfway up one leg of the module.

6.5 m (21 ft)

NEIL ARMSTRONG
(1930–2012)
In 1966, he made his first mission aboard the *Gemini VIII*. He was the first man on the Moon. He left NASA in 1971.

MICHAEL COLLINS
(b. 1930)
He was the third astronaut to perform a spacewalk, during the *Gemini X* mission. He was the command module pilot in *Columbia*.

EDWIN ALDRIN
(b. 1930)
He participated in the training tasks for the *Gemini XIII* mission, and was the second man to walk on the lunar surface.

The Paranal Observatory

The Very Large Telescope (VLT) is the most advanced astronomical observatory in the world. It has four telescopes that make it possible, for example, to see the flame of a candle on the surface of the Moon. It is operated by a scientific consortium from 15 countries, and one of its objectives is to find new worlds around other stars.

DOME
Protects and perceives any climate change through thermal sensors.

WEATHER CONDITIONS
The Cerro Paranal in northern Chile is located in the driest part of the Atacama Desert, where conditions for astronomical observation are extraordinary. It is a mountain 2,635 m (8,645 ft) high and offers nearly 350 cloudless nights per year, with unusually high atmospheric stability.

750 mbar
Air pressure

5–20%
Humidity

–8/25ºC
(18/77ºF)
Average temperature

0.96 kg/m³
Air density

AMAZING FACT

The VLT has enabled astronomers to study violent flares bursting from the supermassive black hole at the centre of the Milky Way galaxy.

Secondary mirror 1.2 m (4 ft) in diameter.

In history

Since ancient times men and women have observed the sky seeking answers. In all great civilizations we find examples of astronomical observatories that made it possible to gather knowledge of the Universe and gradually unravel its secrets.

2500–2000 BCE
STONEHENGE
Located in Wiltshire, England, it is an observatory temple from Neolithic times.

1000 BCE
EL CARACOL
Set in the Mayan city of Chichén Itzá, in what is now Mexico, people worshipped the Sun, Moon and Venus in it.

The complex

Completed in 2006, the very large telescope (VLT) has four reflecting telescopes, 8.2 m (27 ft) in diameter, that can observe objects 4 billion times weaker than can normally be seen with the naked eye. It also has four movable auxiliary telescopes 1.8 m (6 ft) in diameter, which, when combined with the large telescopes, produce what is called interferometry: a simulation of the power of a mirror 16 m (52 ft) in diameter and the resolution of a telescope of 200 m (650 ft), which would be able to distinguish an astronaut on the Moon.

20,000 m² (215,000 sq ft)
Total area

2,365 m (7,760 ft)
Altitude

TELESCOPIC UNITS

Light tunnels for interferometry.

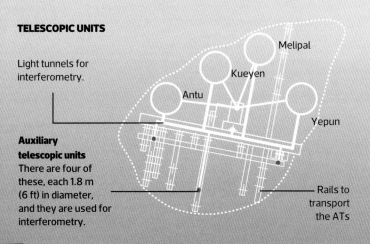

Melipal

Kueyen

Antu

Yepun

Auxiliary telescopic units
There are four of these, each 1.8 m (6 ft) in diameter, and they are used for interferometry.

Rails to transport the ATs

THE TELESCOPE
The main feature of the VLT is its revolutionary optical design. Thanks to the active and adaptive optics, viewers get a resolution similar to being in space.

OPTICAL ADAPTATION
To counteract the blurring effects of the Earth's atmosphere, the VLT has an active optical system featuring 150 pistons that move mirror segments to realign light into sharp images.

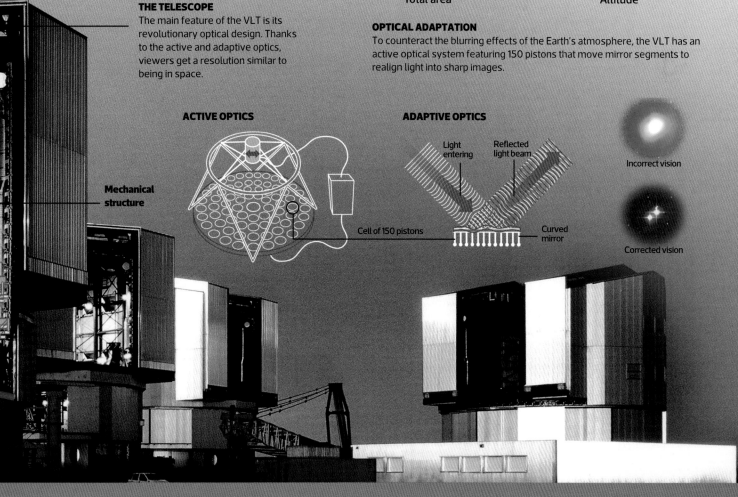

ACTIVE OPTICS

Mechanical structure

Cell of 150 pistons

ADAPTIVE OPTICS

Light entering

Reflected light beam

Curved mirror

Incorrect vision

Corrected vision

1726
JAIPUR
Located in northern India. Built by Maharaja Sawai Jai Singh, it has a large sextant.

1888
LICK
The first to be sited on a high mountain, on the summit of Mount Hamilton, California, at 1,300 m (4,265 ft).

1897
YERKES
In Wisconsin. It contains the largest telescopic lens ever made.

1979
MAUNA KEA
A resort in Hawaii, with UK, French-American and American observatories.

Rockets

Developed in the first half of the twentieth century, rockets are needed to send any device into space. They have enough power to lift their load off the ground and soon acquire the speed needed to escape the effects of gravity and reach outer space.

ARIANE 5

First successful launch	21 October 1998
Diameter	5 m (16 ft)
Total height	51 m (167 ft)
Weight of boosters	277 tons each (full)
Cost of the project	7 billion euros
Maximum load	6,200 kg (13,670 lb)
Organization	ESA

40,320 km/h
(25,054 mph)
Escape velocity of Earth

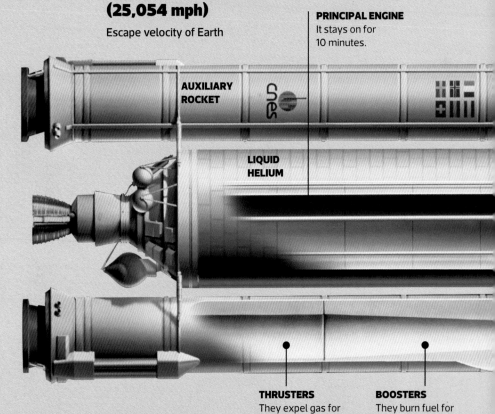

AUXILIARY ROCKET

PRINCIPAL ENGINE
It stays on for 10 minutes.

LIQUID HELIUM

THRUSTERS
They expel gas for the rocket to start its ascent.

BOOSTERS
They burn fuel for two minutes.

70.6 m (232 ft)

51 m (167 ft)

BOEING 747 AIRCRAFT   **ARIANE 5**

1,645,000 lb
(746,000 kg)
Weight on the ground

Operation of the engine

Before take-off, fuel ignition is started. The main engine turns on and only if the ignition is successful the thrusters are turned on. The rocket takes off, and two minutes later the thrusters are turned off when they are out of fuel. The engine stays on for a few minutes and then switches off. A small engine puts the satellite into orbit.

MOTOR

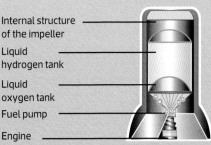

Internal structure of the impeller

Liquid hydrogen tank

Liquid oxygen tank

Fuel pump

Engine

COMPONENT PARTS

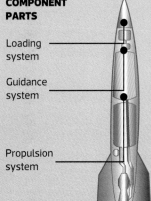

Loading system

Guidance system

Propulsion system

CHEMICALLY POWERED ROCKETS

In liquid-fuel rockets, the liquid hydrogen and oxygen are in separate containers. In solid-fuel rockets, they are mixed and placed in a single cylinder.

Gases removed

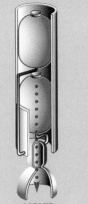  

LIQUID   **SOLID**   **HYBRID**

THERMAL INSULATION

To protect the engine from the high temperatures of the burning fuel in the combustion chamber, the rocket propellant, which is an efficient coolant, is passed through tubes lining the walls of the chamber.

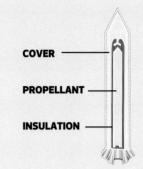

COVER

PROPELLANT

INSULATION

LIQUID HYDROGEN TANK
The main engine weighs 225 tons.

LIQUID OXYGEN TANK
Contains 130 tons for combustion.

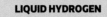

CONNECTOR TUBE

UPPER ENGINES
They release the satellite at exactly the right angle and speed.

LOWER LOAD
Up to two satellites.

UPPER LOAD
Up to two satellites.

NOSE CONE
Protects the load.

How it works

As it rises, the rocket burns fuel and reduces its mass. As the distance from the Earth's surface increases the atmosphere becomes thinner, greatly reducing the effect of air resistance. In addition, the force of gravity diminishes.

ACTION AND REACTION

The thrust of the rocket is the reaction to the action of the burning fuel against the surface.

Thrust of the rocket

Gravity of Earth

TYPE OF ROCKET ACCORDING TO PROPULSION

The chemical propulsion rocket is the most widely used. It is driven by combustion. The nuclear type is driven by fission or fusion. The ion motor provides the possibility of electrically charging atoms by stripping electrons.

Thrust

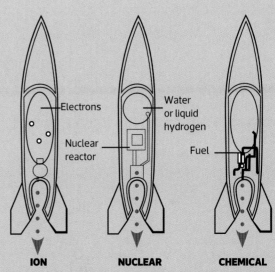

Electrons

Water or liquid hydrogen

Nuclear reactor

Fuel

ION   **NUCLEAR**   **CHEMICAL**

The Space Shuttle

Unlike conventional rockets, the space shuttle could be used over and over again, to launch and repair satellites and as an astronomical laboratory. The US fleet had five space shuttles over its 30-year programme: *Challenger* and *Columbia* (exploded 1986 and 2003 respectively), *Discovery*, *Atlantis* and *Endeavour* (retired 2011). Some of the shuttle's functions will in future be carried out by NASA's planned Space Launch System.

SATELLITE
Stowed in the cargo hold and moved by the mechanical arm.

DISCOVERY

First launch 12–14 April 1981	
Orbital period Between 5 and 20 days	
Wingspan 24 m (79 ft)	
Length 37 m (121 ft)	
Organization NASA	

External fuel tank

Space orbiter

Auxiliary rockets

MECHANICAL ARM
Moved satellites in and out of the cargo module.

11,600 kg
(25,575 lb)
Weight on the ground

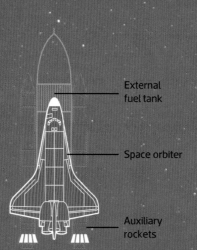

SPACE ORBITER

BOEING 747

SPACE SHUTTLE

37 m (121 ft)

COMMAND CABIN

Cabin

Divided into two levels – an upper one for the pilot and co-pilot (and up to two astronauts), and a lower one where everyday work was done. The habitable volume of the cabin was 70 m³ (2,470 cu ft).

CERAMIC TILES
They were made up of layers that protected the spacecraft from heat.

Skin of orbiter

Adhesive felt

Silica fibre

Vitreous coating

CONTROLS
In the cockpit there were more than 2,000 separate controls.

Control keypad

Control cabin

Pilot's seat

Commander's seat

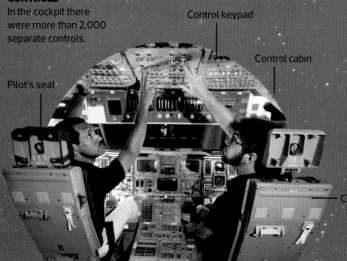

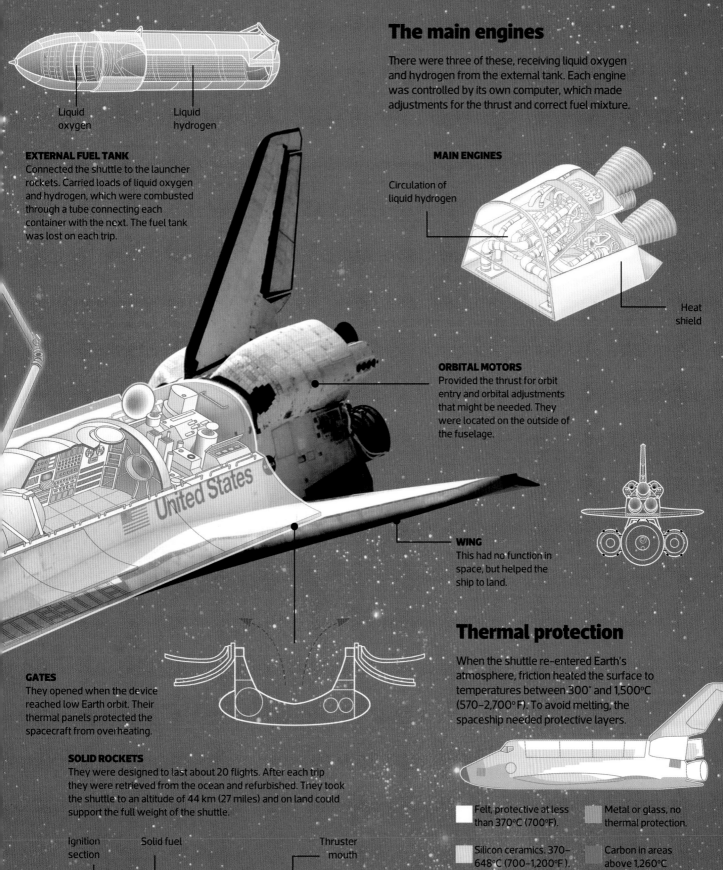

Liquid oxygen

Liquid hydrogen

The main engines

There were three of these, receiving liquid oxygen and hydrogen from the external tank. Each engine was controlled by its own computer, which made adjustments for the thrust and correct fuel mixture.

EXTERNAL FUEL TANK
Connected the shuttle to the launcher rockets. Carried loads of liquid oxygen and hydrogen, which were combusted through a tube connecting each container with the next. The fuel tank was lost on each trip.

MAIN ENGINES

Circulation of liquid hydrogen

Heat shield

ORBITAL MOTORS
Provided the thrust for orbit entry and orbital adjustments that might be needed. They were located on the outside of the fuselage.

WING
This had no function in space, but helped the ship to land.

GATES
They opened when the device reached low Earth orbit. Their thermal panels protected the spacecraft from overheating.

SOLID ROCKETS
They were designed to last about 20 flights. After each trip they were retrieved from the ocean and refurbished. They took the shuttle to an altitude of 44 km (27 miles) and on land could support the full weight of the shuttle.

Ignition section

Solid fuel

Thruster mouth

Thermal protection

When the shuttle re-entered Earth's atmosphere, friction heated the surface to temperatures between 300° and 1,500°C (570–2,700°F). To avoid melting, the spaceship needed protective layers.

Felt, protective at less than 370°C (700°F).

Silicon ceramics. 370–648°C (700–1,200°F).

Also silicon. 648–1260°C (1,200–2,300°F).

Metal or glass, no thermal protection.

Carbon in areas above 1,260°C (2,300°F).

Satellite Orbits

The space available for broadcast satellites is finite and could become saturated. Errors of one or two degrees in terms of location may cause interference between neighbouring satellites. Therefore, their positions are regulated by the International Telecommunication Union (ITU). Geostationary satellites (GEO) maintain a fixed position relative to Earth. In contrast, those in low (LEO) and medium Earth orbit (MEO) require monitoring from ground stations.

Different types

The satellites transmit information of a given quality according to their position in relation to Earth. GEO orbits can cover the entire Earth with only four satellites, while lower orbits (LEO) need constellations of satellites to achieve full coverage. Both LEO and MEO satellites follow elliptical orbits.

ORBITS	LEO	MEO	GEO
Distance from Earth	200–2,000 km (125–1,250 miles)	2,000–36,000 km (1,250–22,400 miles)	36,000 km (22,400 miles)
Cost of satellites	Low	Medium	High
Type of network	Complex	Medium	Simple
Life of satellite	3–7 years	10–15 years	10–15 years
Coverage	Short	Medium	Continuous

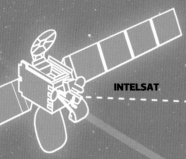

INTELSAT

Polar Orbit

36,000 km (22,400 miles) altitude

GEO ▶

The geostationary orbit is circular. The period of the orbit is 23 hours 56 minutes, the same as that of the Earth. Its most frequent use is for television.

Equatorial orbit

LEO ▶

Low altitude orbit, between 200 and 2,000 km (125 and 1,250 miles), was first used in mobile telephony after the saturation of GEO orbits. The orbits are circular and consume less power, but they require terrestrial centres to track the satellites.

ELLIPTICAL ORBIT

Apogee
Farthest point from Earth.

Perigee
Closest point relative to Earth.

CIRCULAR ORBIT

Equal distance from Earth.

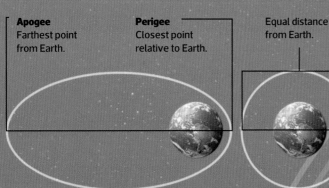

AMAZING FACT

The use of geostationary satellites for telecommunications was predicted by the British science fiction writer, Arthur C. Clarke, in 1945.

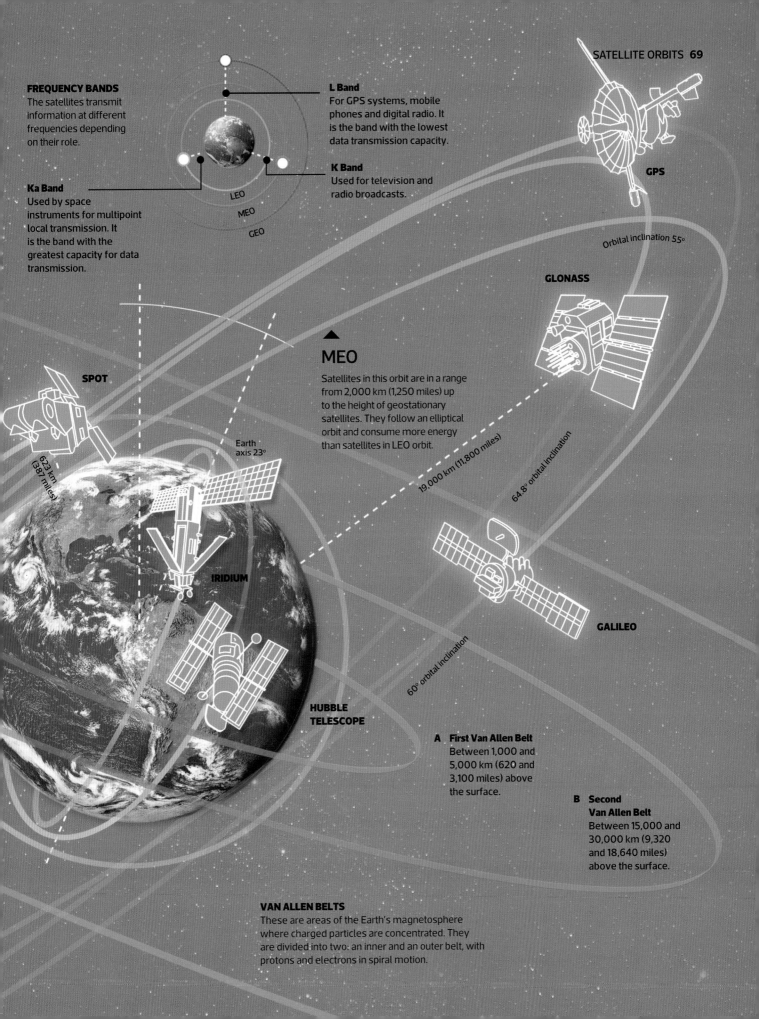

FREQUENCY BANDS
The satellites transmit information at different frequencies depending on their role.

L Band
For GPS systems, mobile phones and digital radio. It is the band with the lowest data transmission capacity.

K Band
Used for television and radio broadcasts.

Ka Band
Used by space instruments for multipoint local transmission. It is the band with the greatest capacity for data transmission.

LEO
MEO
GEO

GPS

Orbital inclination 55°

GLONASS

SPOT

623 km (387 miles)

Earth axis 23°

▲
MEO
Satellites in this orbit are in a range from 2,000 km (1,250 miles) up to the height of geostationary satellites. They follow an elliptical orbit and consume more energy than satellites in LEO orbit.

19,000 km (11,800 miles)

64.8° orbital inclination

IRIDIUM

GALILEO

60° orbital inclination

HUBBLE TELESCOPE

A First Van Allen Belt
Between 1,000 and 5,000 km (620 and 3,100 miles) above the surface.

B Second Van Allen Belt
Between 15,000 and 30,000 km (9,320 and 18,640 miles) above the surface.

VAN ALLEN BELTS
These are areas of the Earth's magnetosphere where charged particles are concentrated. They are divided into two: an inner and an outer belt, with protons and electrons in spiral motion.

Space Probes

Since the first spacecraft, such as *Mariner* in the 1960s, the contribution to science made by space probes has been considerable. Mostly solar powered, these unmanned machines are equipped with sophisticated instruments that make it possible to study planets, moons, comets, asteroids and the Sun in detail. One particularly renowned probe is the *Mars Reconnaissance Orbiter* (MRO), launched to study Mars from close up in 2005.

Mars Reconnaissance Orbiter

The main objective of this orbiting probe is to seek out traces of water on the surface of Mars. It was launched in summer 2005 by NASA and reached Mars on 10 March 2006. The original two-year mission was extended until October 2014 to follow up on earlier discoveries and monitor yearly variations in Mars's atmospheric and surface processes.

116 million km
(72 million miles)

were travelled by the probe on its journey to Mars.

APPROACH TO MARS

It made 500 orbits

C Final orbit
It travelled along an almost circular orbit, suitable for obtaining data.

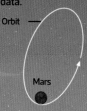

Orbit

Mars

B Braking
To get closer to the planet, the spacecraft slowed down over a six-month period.

A Start
The probe's first orbit travelled along an enormous elliptical path.

Mars's orbit

Earth's orbit

Sun

Earth

Mars

5 Scientific phase
The probe began its analysis phase on the surface of Mars. It found evidence of water.

4 Arrival on Mars
In March 2006, MRO passed into the southern hemisphere of Mars. The probe slowed down considerably.

3 Path correction
Four manoeuvres were made to ensure the correct orbit was reached.

2 Cruising
The probe travelled for seven and a half months before reaching Mars.

1 Launch
Took place on 12 August 2005, from Cape Canaveral, Florida.

1,031 kg
(2,273 lb)

Weight on Earth

AMAZING FACT

Mars is often described as the 'red planet' because much of its surface is covered in fine iron oxide dust, which gives it a rusty appearance.

TECHNICAL DATA

Weight with fuel	2,180 kg (4,806 lb)
Panel resistance	Up to -200° C (-328° F)
Launch rocket	Atlas V-401
Duration of the mission	Nine years
Cost	US $720 million

MRO   MGS   Odyssey

On Mars

The main objective of the *MRO* was to find evidence of water on the surface of Mars, to help explain the evolution of the planet. The probe's devices facilitate high-resolution imagery of the surface and analysis of minerals. It has also created daily climatic maps of Mars.

3,744

cells on each panel convert solar energy into electricity.

SOLAR PANELS
The probe's main power source is the Sun. The craft has two solar panels with a total surface area of 40 m² (430 sq ft).

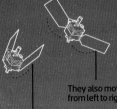

Opening the panels
The panels are opened while in orbit.

They also move from left to right.

Once unfolded, they use an axis.

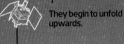

They begin to unfold upwards.

The panels are almost closed.

SHARAD RADAR

SOLAR PANEL

HIGH-GAIN PARABOLIC ANTENNA
Its data transfer capacity is ten times greater than the capacity of previous orbiters.

SOLAR PANEL

INSTRUMENTS
Used at the same time, HiRISE, CTX and CRISM offer very high quality information about a given area.

HiRISE high-resolution camera
Provides details on geological structures and has considerably improved resolution compared with previous missions.

MGS
Observes Mars's atmosphere.

MARCI
Provides the images with colour.

CRISM Spectrometer
Divides visible and infrared light in the images into various colours that identify different minerals.

CTX Context Camera
Offers panoramic views that help to provide context to the images captured by HiRISE and CRISM.

HiRISE
Mars Reconnaissance Orbiter (2005)

MGS
Mars Global Surveyor (1996)

30 cm (12 in)/pixel

150 cm (60 in)/pixel

HiRISE   **CRISM**   **CTX**

The type of image taken by the CTX, which helps to provide context for an image taken by HiRISE.

Detailed image taken by HiRISE.

Space Stations

Life on space stations makes it possible to study the effects of remaining in outer space for long periods of time, while providing an environment for carrying out scientific experiments in laboratories. These stations are equipped with systems that provide the crew with oxygen and filter their exhaled carbon dioxide.

Orbit
The ISS performs around 16 complete orbits of the Earth each day, at a height of between 335 and 460 km (208–286 miles).

The ISS

The International Space Station (ISS) is the result of the merger of NASA's *Freedom* project with *Mir-2*, run by the Russian Federal Space Agency (RKA). Construction started in 1998 and to this day it continues to expand, using modules provided by countries across the globe. Its inhabitable surface area is equal to that of a Boeing 747.

PROVISION AND WASTE
The Russian spacecraft ATV connects to the ISS, to provide supplies and remove waste.

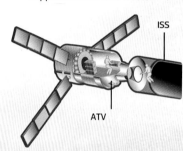

ISS

ATV

TECHNICAL INFORMATION

Inhabitable space	837 m³ (29,560 cu ft)
Speed	27,700 km/h (17,200 mph)
Measurements	110 x 100 x 30 m (360 x 330 x 100 ft)
Surface area of the panels	4,000 m² (43,000 sq ft)
Laboratories	6
Production	USA, Russia, Japan, EU, Canada

ZVEZDA MODULE
The main Russian contribution to the station, the first living space. It houses three to seven astronauts.

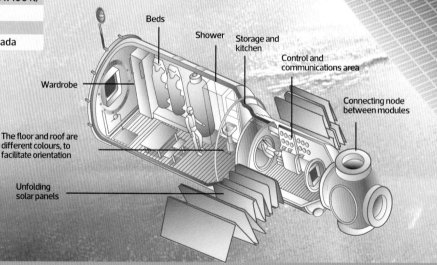

Beds

Shower

Storage and kitchen

Control and communications area

Wardrobe

Connecting node between modules

The floor and roof are different colours, to facilitate orientation

Unfolding solar panels

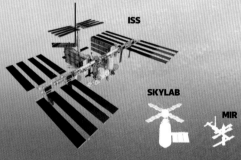

ZVEZDA module

ISS

SKYLAB

MIR

PHASES OF CONSTRUCTION

NOVEMBER 1998
Zarya module
First sector put into orbit. It powered the first construction stages of the ISS.

DECEMBER 1998
Unity module
Connection finger between the living and working area modules. Provided by the EU.

JULY 2000
Zvezda module
The structural and functional heart of the ISS. Fully built and put into orbit by Russia.

OCTOBER 2000
Z1 Truss and Ku–Band antenna
Neutralizes the static electricity generated in the ISS and facilitates communication with Earth.

NOVEMBER 2000
P6 Truss
Structural module that features radiators to disperse the heat generated in the station.

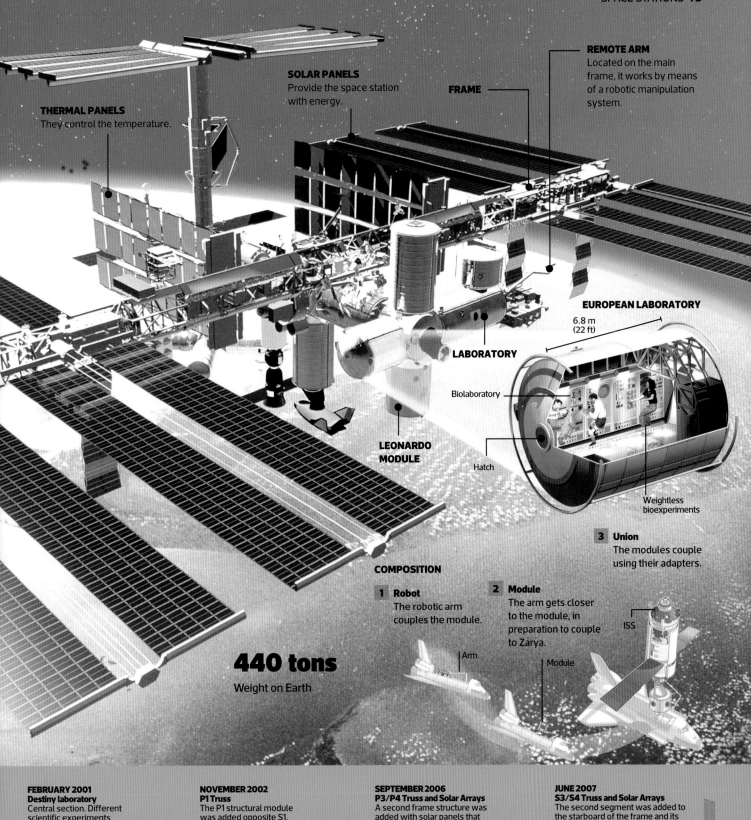

THERMAL PANELS
They control the temperature.

SOLAR PANELS
Provide the space station with energy.

FRAME

REMOTE ARM
Located on the main frame, it works by means of a robotic manipulation system.

EUROPEAN LABORATORY

6.8 m
(22 ft)

LABORATORY

Biolaboratory

LEONARDO MODULE

Hatch

Weightless bioexperiments

440 tons
Weight on Earth

COMPOSITION

1 Robot
The robotic arm couples the module.

2 Module
The arm gets closer to the module, in preparation to couple to Zarya.

3 Union
The modules couple using their adapters.

Arm

Module

ISS

FEBRUARY 2001
Destiny laboratory
Central section. Different scientific experiments are performed in a zero-gravity environment.

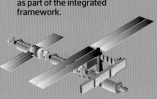

NOVEMBER 2002
P1 Truss
The P1 structural module was added opposite S1, as part of the integrated framework.

SEPTEMBER 2006
P3/P4 Truss and Solar Arrays
A second frame structure was added with solar panels that has meant the station is self-sufficient in terms of power.

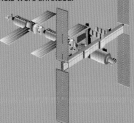

JUNE 2007
S3/S4 Truss and Solar Arrays
The second segment was added to the starboard of the frame and its solar panels were unfolded.

The Hubble Telescope

Space telescopes are artificial satellites sent into orbit to explore different areas of the Universe, avoiding the effects of atmospheric turbulence that affect the quality of images. Hubble, put into orbit on 25 April 1990 by NASA and ESA, is managed by remote control, operated by astronomers in several countries.

Accurate cameras

On the Hubble space telescope, the place of human observers is occupied by sensitive light detectors and cameras that photograph views of the cosmos. In 1993, after the discovery of a fault with its main mirror, corrective lenses (COSTAR) were installed to correct its focus.

11,100 kg
(24,500 lb)

Weight on Earth

ENTRANCE
Opened during observations to allow light to enter.

TECHNICAL DATA

Launch date	25 April 1990
Orbital height	600 km (373 miles)
Orbital period	97 minutes
Type of telescope	Ritchey–Chrétien Reflector
Organization	NASA and ESA
Launch cost	US $2 billion
Diameter of the primary mirror	2.4 m (8 ft)

14 m (46 ft)

4.26 m (14 ft)

OUTER COVER
Protects the telescope from the effects of outer space.

SECONDARY MIRROR
After being reflected here, light reaches the camera.

WIDE FIELD PLANETARY CAMERA (WFPC)
Main electronic camera.

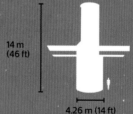

HOW IMAGES ARE CAPTURED

Hubble uses a system of mirrors that capture light and converge it until it becomes focused.

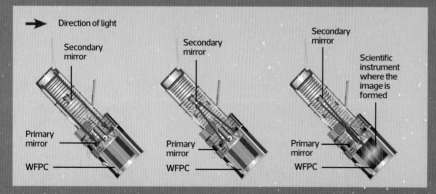

Direction of light

Secondary mirror

Secondary mirror

Secondary mirror

Scientific instrument where the image is formed

Primary mirror

WFPC

Primary mirror

WFPC

Primary mirror

WFPC

1 Entrance of light
Light enters through the opening and reflects against the primary mirror.

2 Light ricochet
The light then converges towards the secondary mirror, which returns it to the primary mirror.

3 Image formed
The rays of light concentrate on the focal plane, where the image is formed.

HOW IMAGES ARE TRANSMITTED

1 Hubble
It selects the target and processes it to obtain data.

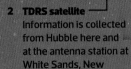

2 TDRS satellite
Information is collected from Hubble here and at the antenna station at White Sands, New Mexico, USA.

3 Earth
From New Mexico, the information is transmitted to Goddard Space Flight Center in Greenbelt, Maryland, USA, where it is analysed.

IMAGES
As they are taken outside the Earth's atmosphere, the clarity of images produced by Hubble is much better than those taken from telescopes on Earth.

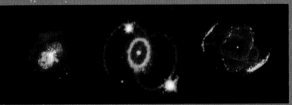

ETA CARINAE STAR **SUPERNOVA** **CAT'S EYE NEBULA**

HIGH-GAIN ANTENNA
It receives orders from Earth and returns photographs as TV signals.

SOLAR PANEL
Power is provided by means of directional solar antennae.

PRIMARY, OR MAIN, MIRROR
Measuring 2.4 m (8 ft) in diameter, it captures and focuses light.

COSTAR
Optics device that corrected the original defective mirror fitted on Hubble.

CAMERA FOR BLURRY OBJECTS

OTHER TELESCOPES

CHANDRA
Launched in 1999, it is NASA's main X-ray observatory.

SOHO
Developed jointly by NASA and ESA, it allows scientists to view interactions between the Sun and Earth in detail. Placed in orbit in 1995.

SPITZER
Launched in August 2003, it observes the Universe in infrared light.

Voyager Probes

The *Voyager 1* and *2* space probes were launched by NASA to study the outer Solar System. Launched in 1977, they reached Saturn in 1980 and Neptune in 1989, and they are currently continuing on their journey beyond the Solar System. Both probes have become the farthest-reaching artificial instruments launched by humankind into space.

PIONEER 10 AND 11
Pioneer 10 was the first spacecraft to perform a flyby of Jupiter, in 1973, and to study Saturn, in 1979. It was followed by *Pioneer 11* in 1974, which lost communication in 1995.

Voyager Interstellar Mission

When *Voyager 1* and *2* left the Solar System, the project was renamed the Voyager Interstellar Mission. Both probes continue to study the fields that they detect.

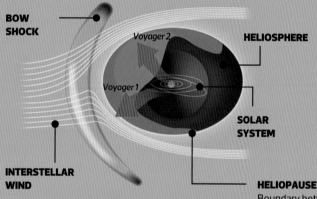

BOW SHOCK

Voyager 2

HELIOSPHERE

Voyager 1

SOLAR SYSTEM

INTERSTELLAR WIND

HELIOPAUSE
Boundary between the area of the Sun's influence and outer space.

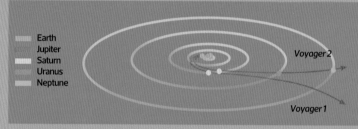

Earth
Jupiter
Saturn
Uranus
Neptune

Voyager 2

Voyager 1

TRAJECTORY
The *Voyager 1* probe passed by Jupiter in 1979 and by Saturn in 1980. *Voyager 2* did the same and arrived at Uranus in 1986, and Neptune in 1989. Both are still active.

BEYOND THE SOLAR SYSTEM
Once outside the heliopause, *Voyager* can measure waves that escape the Sun's magnetic field, from the so-called bow shock, an area where solar winds suddenly decrease due to the disappearance of the Sun's magnetic field.

AMAZING FACT

New Horizons was launched by NASA in 2006 to study Pluto and the Kuiper Belt, and is expected to become the fifth interstellar probe.

LANDMARKS

1977
Launches
Voyager 1 and *2* were launched by NASA from Cape Canaveral in Florida, marking the beginning of a long, successful mission that is still ongoing.

1977
Photo of the Earth and the Moon
On 5 September, *Voyager 1* sent photographs of the Earth and the Moon, demonstrating that it was fully functional.

1986
Uranus encounter
Voyager 2 reached Uranus on 24 January. It sent back photographs of the planet and measurements of its satellites, rings and magnetic fields.

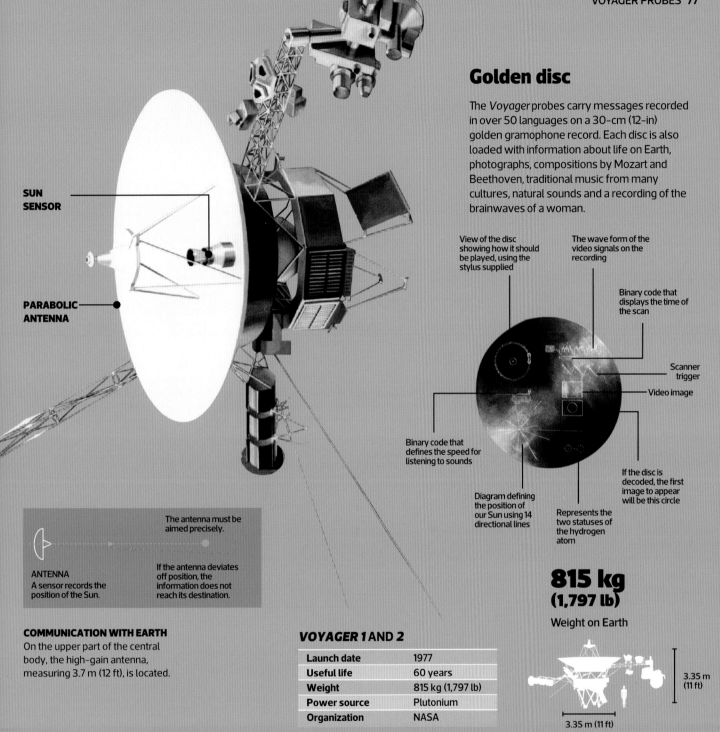

SUN
SENSOR

PARABOLIC
ANTENNA

Golden disc

The *Voyager* probes carry messages recorded in over 50 languages on a 30-cm (12-in) golden gramophone record. Each disc is also loaded with information about life on Earth, photographs, compositions by Mozart and Beethoven, traditional music from many cultures, natural sounds and a recording of the brainwaves of a woman.

View of the disc showing how it should be played, using the stylus supplied

The wave form of the video signals on the recording

Binary code that displays the time of the scan

Scanner trigger

Video image

Binary code that defines the speed for listening to sounds

If the disc is decoded, the first image to appear will be this circle

Diagram defining the position of our Sun using 14 directional lines

Represents the two statuses of the hydrogen atom

The antenna must be aimed precisely.

ANTENNA
A sensor records the position of the Sun.

If the antenna deviates off position, the information does not reach its destination.

COMMUNICATION WITH EARTH
On the upper part of the central body, the high-gain antenna, measuring 3.7 m (12 ft), is located.

815 kg
(1,797 lb)

Weight on Earth

3.35 m (11 ft)

3.35 m (11 ft)

VOYAGER 1 AND 2

Launch date	1977
Useful life	60 years
Weight	815 kg (1,797 lb)
Power source	Plutonium
Organization	NASA

1987
Observation of a supernova
Supernova 1987A appeared in the Large Magellanic Cloud. A high-quality photograph was taken by *Voyager 2*.

1989
Colour photo of Neptune
Voyager 2 was the first spacecraft to observe Neptune. It also photographed its largest moon, Triton, from close up.

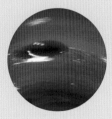

1998
Beating the record set by *Pioneer 10*
Pioneer 10 flew past Jupiter in 1973. On 17 February, *Voyager 1* passed Jupiter, and reached farther than any other spacecraft.

Space Debris

Since the launch of the first satellite in 1957, the space around Earth has become littered by a huge amount of debris. Spent satellite batteries, parts of rockets and spacecraft orbit around Earth. The danger of these objects' presence is the possibility of a collision: they travel at speeds ranging from 30,000 to 70,000 km/h (18,640–43,500 mph).

Cosmic rubbish

Any useless, artificial object that orbits Earth is considered space debris. Rockets used just once continue to orbit the planet, as do bits of spacecraft or devices intentionally destroyed so that they do not move into incorrect orbits.

THE SIZE OF SPACE DEBRIS
More than 11,000 catalogued objects have been accumulated, in addition to millions of tiny particles.

+30,000,000
Measure less than 1 cm (0.4 in)
Very small particles cause limited surface damage.

+100,000
Measure between 1 cm and 10 cm (0.4–4 in)
Particles that can create holes in satellites.

+11,000
Measure more than 10 cm (4 in)
Capable of causing irreparable damage. They have been catalogued and are monitored from Earth.

OBJECTS IN SPACE BY COUNTRY
Since 1957, 25,000 objects have been launched into low orbit. Most come from Russia and the USA.

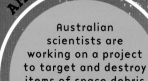

AMAZING FACT

Australian scientists are working on a project to target and destroy items of space debris using giant lasers fired from Earth.

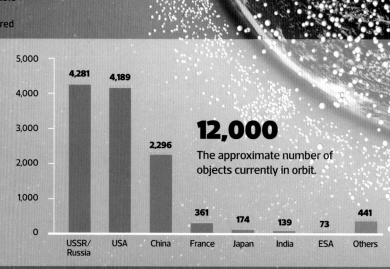

12,000
The approximate number of objects currently in orbit.

USSR/Russia	4,281	
USA	4,189	
China	2,296	
France	361	
Japan	174	
India	139	
ESA	73	
Others	441	

What can we do?

One solution could be to return all debris to Earth, rather than leaving it orbiting around the planet. However, the current intention is to work on satellite debris to remove it from Earth's orbit.

Sail
Just like on a boat, the sail is released when the satellite stops working and the solar winds divert it.

Space probe
It impacts against the satellite, which is diverted from its orbit and driven in a pre-established direction.

Cable
A cable drags the satellite to lower orbits. It disintegrates when entering the atmosphere.

SOURCE AND LOCATION

Ninety-five per cent of objects in orbit around Earth are considered 'space waste'. NASA is studying a way of using rockets that do not reach orbit and will return to Earth, avoiding the creation of more waste.

21 per cent inactive satellites

5 per cent active satellites

31 per cent rockets and rocket boosters

43 per cent fragments of satellites

2,000 tons

of rubbish are orbiting at less than 2,000 km (1,250 miles).

HIGH ORBIT
100,000 KM (62,000 MILES)
Astronomic satellites operate at the highest orbit.

LOW EARTH ORBIT
200–2,000 KM (125–1,250 MILES)
The International Space Station, the Hubble telescope and telecommunication satellites orbit here.

GEOSTATIONARY ORBIT
36,000 KM (22,400 MILES)
Spy satellites, which generate a significant amount of waste.

Waste
Functional
Nuclear spills

Index